BLACK FIRE ON

CONTRAVERSIONS
CRITICAL STUDIES IN JEWISH LITERATURE,
CULTURE, AND SOCIETY

Daniel Boyarin and Chana Kronfeld
General Editors

BLACK FIRE
ON WHITE FIRE

AN ESSAY ON JEWISH HERMENEUTICS, FROM MIDRASH TO KABBALAH

BETTY ROJTMAN

Translated by Steven Rendall

University of California Press

Berkeley · Los Angeles · London

The publisher gratefully acknowledges the contribution provided by the General Endowment Fund, which is supported by generous gifts from the members of the Associates of the University of California Press.

The publisher gratefully acknowledges the contributions of the French Ministry of Culture in the publication of this book.

The author wishes to acknowledge the assistance of the Department for Torah Education and Culture in the Diaspora, the World Zionist Organization, in the publication of this book.

This book was originally published as *Feu noir sur feu blanc* by Editions Verdier, 1986.

University of California Press
Berkeley and Los Angeles, California

University of California Press
London, England

Library of Congress Cataloging-in-Publication Data
Rojtman, Betty.
    [Feu noir sur feu blanc. English]
    Black fire on white fire : an essay on Jewish hermeneutics: from midrash to kabbalah / Betty Rojtman; translated by Steven Rendall.
        p.   cm. — (Contraversions; 10)
    Includes bibliographical references and index.
        ISBN 0–520–20320–8 (cloth: alk. paper). — ISBN 0–520–20321–6 (pbk.: alk. paper)
    1. Bible. O.T.—Criticism, interpretation, etc., Jewish.
    2. Bible. O.T.—Hermeneutics.   I. Title.   II. Series.
BS1186.R6513   1998
296.1—dc21   97–3010
                                                                    CIP
                                                                    r97

Printed in the United States of America

This book is a print-on-demand volume. It is manufactured using toner in place of ink. Type and images may be less sharp than the same material seen in traditionally printed University of California editions.

The paper used in this publication meets the minimum requirements of ANSI/NISO Z39.48 – 1992 (R 1997) (Permanence of paper)

To the memory of my grandfather,
Nathan Pin'has ben Avraham Alexander Schleider

Contents

Preface

Jewish culture, like any literary tradition based on canonic writings, is haunted by the problem of validating later developments against its earlier, authoritative formulations. This necessitates not only exegetical efforts to clarify the texts against the more recent theological developments but sometimes also more literary approaches to the canonic texts, informed by new rhetoric and by more complex and systematic grammatical assumptions. Canonic texts were arranged and rearranged according to various criteria, in attempts to validate both the exegete's thought and the validity and relevance of the canon. Theological coherence and grammatical stability were rarely a main concern of the biblical and rabbinic masters. Their projects were oriented toward shaping other forms of stability, ritualistic and ethical ones, which were believed to be and were presented as religiously compelling ways of behavior. Provided that this was the cultural choice of the ancient Jewish elites, it was a dramatic shift that the Middle Ages contributed to Jewish thought. Less associative and less mythical thinkers appeared within Jewish culture, most of them striving to offer pictures of coherence that, different as they are, nevertheless suggest efforts to impose forms of order on the more chaotic material they revered and to which they attempted to offer the most generous interpretations possible.

This search for inserting relative order into a relative textual chaos was resisted from time to time by more traditional Jewish authors. Only rarely were they systematic philosophers, or immersed in systematic grammatical studies. These two fields remained beyond the scope of most of the Jewish traditional literature, which preferred the cohesiveness of a way of life to the coherence of the way of thought or even of the canonic text. Imposing order was, however, a problematic enterprise because of the intellectual diversity of the sources that constitute the canons, both the biblical and the rabbinic ones. The new forms of organization also meant exclusion, misinterpretation, and overemphasis. New theological dictionaries emerged, as is the case with the medieval treatments of the divine attributes shown in the first part of Maimonides' *Guide of the Perplexed*, or in the innumerable commentaries on the ten *sefirot* in Kabbalah.

The competing projects, which at times may be conceived as reactions to each other, created tensions, frictions, controversies, and eventually even mutual accusations of heresy. The efforts to offer syntheses of the more mythical and the more systematic ways of thinking also created some confusions, as they combined divergent ways of thought into what may be conceived as rather superficial concordances. Systematic thinking and the conceptual content of the new approaches created some order for a few and more confusion for many. All this provided that there is no need to deny forms of coherence that transcend the ritualistic. Language itself, mythical as it may be, displays by its very nature and creates by its very communicative role a sense of commonality, of cohesion and coherence. To the natural sense of order involved in language and in the practice of a group, additional types of conceptual order were added by medieval and later thinkers. Some detected implicit principles that organize the discourse even if they are explicit in the interpreted texts or elsewhere. This is the case for both the philosophical and the kabbalistic hermeneutics, which, given the unsystematic nature of the earlier wish forms of literature, had to be formulated for the first time by the later thinkers. In fact, even the hermeneutical discussions of the Middle Age corpora offer quite new aspects, totally absent in the much more cultivated topic of rules for interpretations found in rabbinic literature: strong allegorical and a variety of symbolic exegetical modes had been explicated, based on the practice of importing within the ancient texts metaphysical constellations that informed the religious life of the medieval authors. I propose to call this import an intercorporal approach, since the explanation of the canonic texts was provided by resorting to external concepts stemming from literary corpora alien to the interpreted texts. However, there are important instances of what I propose to designate as the intracorporal exegesis which attempt to clarify the meaning of a corpus by sustained comparison of one part of the corpus to the other, and importing the meanings found in one segment of the corpus into the other. Or, as Rojtman insightfully formulated it, the Bible is its own norm. By definition, this is a less conceptual approach than the intercorporal approach that, by definition, creates encounters between different forms of thought. An important example of the intercorporal approach is offered by Rojtman's study.

Its title, drawing from a famous dictum about the nature of the primordial Torah as written on a background of white fire, is part of the attempt to offer a unique status to the canonic text, which was conceived as preexistent, and according to some versions of this dictum, this white fire is no other than the skin of God, so that the canonic text was conceived as literally divine. This assumption, later developed in the kabbalistic hermeneutics, encouraged an intracorporal approach by ancient and medieval exegetes. The belief in the perfection of the text allowed a more intense examination of components of the text, whose semantic cargo is normally less important, as fraught with significance. Rojtman's study inscribes itself in a very fruitful manner both in the systemic approach of the medieval Jewish thinkers and the intracorporal approach that characterizes many stages of Jewish hermeneutics. Rojtman shows how the metaphysical constellation of the ten *sefirot* serves as an organizing factor for the demonstrative pronouns in the Bible, with a special emphasis on the feminine demonstrative *zot*, which was conceived to point to the last *sefirah*, Malkhut. This is a fresh and important contribution to Jewish hermeneutics, as it attempts to formulate the logic of development from the biblical material to more and more complex exegetical approaches, which culminate in the symbolism of Kabbalah.

Rojtman presupposes a continuous growth of hermeneutical thinking, moving from ancient to medieval and even modern Hasidic texts, and she addresses her sources with sympathy and understanding.

Moshe Idel
Hebrew University

BLACK FIRE ON WHITE FIRE

Introduction

And God's writing was on the Tables,
"Black fire on white fire."
                              Tan'huma, Genesis 1

The narrative of the Torah given by God to Moses opens with
the second letter of the alphabet, the *beth* of plurality.[1] The
Law of truth, the charter of the world's foundation, is thus
presented first of all as disseminated Word at the heart of the
unique—as if the divine message in Jewish monotheism were
delivered a priori in the mode of the multiple, in accord with a
constitutive internal doubling between Written Law and Oral
Law, between the first and second Tables. This repetition of the
same deliberately *sidesteps* any coincidence: as a deep rent in
the fabric of an absolute pronouncement, it marks the entire
range of the history to come, the place allowed for the living
within an essential Word.

Exegesis repeats this paradox in elucidating the text of the
Bible: it posits a true, univocal meaning that nevertheless opens
out toward the world and "plays" between writing and orality, between the interpreted word and the transmitted word.
Engraved on the Tables by God's finger, the letters of His Decalog, the Mishnah tells us,[2] still indicate the path of a kind of lib-
erty. The principle of Revelation, which gives the spirit *along
with* the letter, does not exclude the possibility of *hidush*, or renewal of signification.

Moses has already been told everything on Sinai, and yet
everything has still to be begun: the Talmud assumes[3] that a
student familiar with studying (*talmid vatik*), who has mas-
tered the tradition, will naturally be led to reread—"in the
future"—this text and its "blanks," and to (re)discover in it an

1

undeciphered, radically new meaning, whose reading was nevertheless *already* included in the word revealed to Moses on Mount Sinai.

This semantic indeterminacy seems to proceed from the very absolute that bears it: the Torah functions as a "deictic text,"[4] *manifesting* its own expectation of an actualization still to come. Each addressee, "having to reflect that he himself came out of Egypt,"[5] authenticates the projection onto the text of his own existential coefficient.

EXEGETICAL PRINCIPLES

The transformation of meanings in exegesis will thus resemble an arithmetical series: infinite, but secretly calculated, finally folded back on the structure that produces it. Hermeneutic *praxis* repeats this dialectical principle in accord with differing interpretive modules.

ORALITY

The first perspective is that of *orality*. According to the Word's intention at the origin, the divine message was supposed to be wholly present in the first world of the Decalog, the Anokhi ("I") of pure essence. Writing consecrates man's fault and his stumbling when confronted by the unfinished, by the inherent ambiguity of oral memory.

Tradition considers any writing, any fixed elucidation, as a restriction of thought with respect to the breadth of its original project. Many midrashim[6] recount the priority and primacy of the voice over the text.[7]

Writing is the abdication, the regression of sense into the rigidity of the written word. Something of its original plasticity is inscribed in the text of the Bible: *consonantal* and incomplete, Hebraic writing is realized in vocalization. The score of a song whose vowels determine the diction, always actualized, always taken up again and different from itself, the Torah is presented as a call by the text itself, which bears witness, even in its typographical "blank white spaces," to a "void" in which the sense finds its inspiration. At the origin of speech, this white space was fire, mingled with the black fire of letters: "The Law that God gave to Moses was written in black fire on white fire."[8]

The two concurrent sources constituted by the written text and the "sung" or "chanted" text are maintained in parallel and opposed in a voluntarily unresolved antinomy. "The norm of text is sometimes that of the tradition, sometimes that of reading": Em lamasoreth, ve'em lamikrah.[9] Rejecting the hypothesis of some sort of scribal error, the tradition prefers to respect an ambivalence that is necessary as such, assuming and symbolizing the natural mutations of reading through time, the *deviation* inherent in transmission.

DISSEMINATION

The second opening toward a "labor" of the text—in the sense in which women labor in giving birth—arises from the *rejection of systematization* inherent in rabbinical exegesis. For instance, it took centuries—following the rhythm of the future moving on (halakhah)—to codify the jurisprudence of Hebrew law.

The Talmud itself appears as a unity homogeneous in content but analytic in its conclusions. The text seems to have "caught" the exegetical discussions in a sort of instantaneous lava flow, together with the contradictions, digressions, and dead ends they bear along with them. Divided up by readings, the textual abundance is broken into partial perspectives.

Each structuration thus constitutes one of the seventy facets of the Torah,[10] each of which has an infinite number of reflections. "Each and all" are recognized as authentic, as "words of the living God"[11]—of the God of Life in the process of living.

Here again, arbitrariness is limited by tradition: underlying the commentaries as a whole, an objective coherence inspires and directs interpretation. This coherence nevertheless remains implicit: it cannot and must not be grasped as a whole and is deformed in being expressed. It is an "absent structure," totalizing—but hidden; touched upon, but not attained; always true and false in its multiple approximations.

Modernity has more often risked such syntheses, sacrificing an original baroque signification in the interest of linear clarity. Any settled determination of the sense, no matter how scrupulous and well-founded it may be, runs counter to traditional Jewish sensibility; it could proceed only from a pedagogical concern responding to the demands of the time; it acknowledges the necessary limits of its project: the reading of a period and the loss of sense in its structuration.[12]

The Hermeneutic Process

In addition to these indeterminacies there is also the indeterminacy of the hermeneutic process itself, which proceeds in ambiguous ways.

If the oral Law brings to the individual statement its multiple traditions of reading, the generation of the sense that unites them remains problematic. The role of interpretation is to combine units from differing systems, to link the textual with the ritual, written characters with existential significations.

Within these objective limits, the circulation of sense is free, both on the logical level (the Law has thirteen deductive modes,[13] the Narrative has thirty-two[14]) and on the linguistic level (the rules of language are not fixed by tradition).

Provided that the integrity of this vast puzzle represented by the hermeneutic material and composed of forms of language and forms of thought is guaranteed, the exegete who controls its arrangement is allowed to choose among the infinite number of possible ways of constructing it.

We should remember in particular an indeterminacy of the (axial) meaning and "place" of exegesis, which can be conceived both as moving from the Written Law to the Oral Law, or inversely, from the tradition to the text: "However, there are many commentaries whose first cause will be difficult to determine: did the commentators initially want to explain a difficult verse, in a spontaneous and somewhat arbitrary manner, or did they use the verse as pretext for expressing their point of view? . . . and perhaps these two ways of proceeding are mixed up together."[15]

There is also the indeterminacy of the point at which the exegesis is connected with the statement, which permits the Talmud to attach the same conclusions to different contexts. It frequently happens, for instance, that a more "profitable" link is substituted for an earlier relation between text and code, with the sole end of "freeing" the term or determination in question so that it can enter into new relationships.

It nonetheless seems, through another reversal, that exegesis is partially focused on certain privileged contexts in which oral transmission has traced the memory of an occulted significance. For example, the *gezerah shavah*, a discursive principle based on a textual equivalency, "is not left to the free intervention of the reader"; rather, traditional memory limits its application to selected verses.[16]

THE METHOD OF COMMENTARY

This uncertainty principle—situated between precise boundaries—will allow us to lay the methodological foundations of commentary. Jewish exegesis has constructed for itself an entire hermeneutic apparatus that regulates these relations between textual premises and existential conclusions, between original formulations and semantic translations.

These rules, which are more or less explicitly elaborated, respond in turn to the double requirement of logic and tradition: that is, on one hand, to the mathematical laws of the universal, and, on the other, to the particular conventions of a revealed message. The free reasoning of the logician is taken up into a system of signification that transcends it without disconfirming it.

The linguistic sensibility of the rabbis must be situated within this framework. Whether it is a pretext or a stimulus, the text remains the supreme arena for commentary, the ultimate reference of all teaching.

The role played in hermeneutic elaboration by the analysis of language and the acknowledgment of its functions can be understood in this way. Exegesis "turns over the text"[17] to bring out all its subtleties, to exploit all its resources. However, the linguistics on which this procedure is based is itself ambiguous, in that it participates in the same fundamental ambivalence, combining the objective mechanisms of any language with the ideological imperatives to which they are linked.

At its origin is the postulate of the Mosaic revelation: the exegetical grammar is applicable only to the text of the Torah, and its logic is in the end subjected to the hazards of an order of values superior to it. Interpretation hesitates between these two poles, between the sacred text and the living message, in accord with linguistic equations of variable proportions.

THE PROBLEM OF THE NORM

As a vehicle of revelation, biblical discourse must be considered an idiolect; as such it is opaque, its categories remain peculiar to it. Above all, it defines its own laws and is not subject to any external measure of its levels of language. As a "form-standard," *the Bible is its own norm.*

Therefore, *by definition,* one cannot speak of linguistic *anomaly.* Such an anomaly could be established only experimentally, on an essentially statistical basis. It derives from an initial, incomplete, and inadequate description of the Torah's message, whose coherence it fails to grasp. It then becomes a matter of finding a level of reading that reduces this questioning and integrates its irregularity.[18]

The elements of grammatical structuration are always at issue and are continually composed and recomposed, in such a way as to account for a maximum of linguistic facts in relation to a maximum of traditional facts. The rabbis will thus redefine the logic of the text on each occasion, in accord with the chosen interpretive perspective.

Thus, for example, the word *zot,* "this" or "this one," is read as neuter or as feminine depending on whether the exegete prefers, in a particular context, a normal grammatical usage or, on the contrary, an "abnormal" one that then requires justification.

Irregularity thus becomes a notion secreted by reading and measured by its conventions. Its mode of apprehension appears to be ultimately pedagogical: it will be understood as the *gap* between the statement and the reader's cultural expectation, normalization always proceeding in accord with the text; it is indeed our *inadequacy*, not a given unusual formation in the narrative, that is put in question by punctual commentary.

PERFECTION OF EXPRESSION

The second postulate of hermeneutic linguistics is that of an absolute plenitude of form: it guarantees that the discourse will have a maximum density of signification, a saturation of sense in expression. From this is derived a double principle of *economy* and *precision* that determines, at variable thresholds, the exegete's questioning of the text.

The Principle of Economy
(Presence/Absence of the Sign)

As "holy," biblical language also functions as a "full" language that is absolutely economical, in which every redundancy, once it is taken up and explained by exegesis, is no longer merely redundant but *signifies*.[19] Thus interpretation is concerned with the number of occurrences of a term, or even with its appearance in a given context.

Malbim,[20] who in the nineteenth century wrote a kind of semantic treatise on the Bible (*Ayeleth Hashahar*),[21] formulates the principle in these terms: "God's Torah is *perfect*, its form integral, with neither excess nor lack. And in the case of every turn of phrase that appears too long or superfluous, our Sages have explained the necessity of its use and explained its teaching."

Here again, however, the *threshold* of redundancy remains to be defined: everything is essential, but the terms (less numerous or different) in which the essential thing might have been said remained to be determined. As early as the talmudic period, the two great Tanna'im[22] Rabbi Akiva and Rabbi Yishma'el represented the opposite poles in this debate.[23] Rabbi

Yishma'el takes into consideration the stylistic element necessary in every language: "Addressing itself to men" (Diberah Torah kileshon bené adam),[24] the Torah spoke "the language of men": that is, a language in which *rhetoric* is a constituent part of the message. This approach will thus not comment on "idiomatic" expressions, such as the one that attaches a verb root to the corresponding conjugated form ("know—you will know that your posterity will sojourn in a strange land");[25] this occurs too frequently in the Hebrew biblical text to warrant comment.

At the opposite pole from this point of view, Rabbi Akiva interprets even the form of the letters, even the signs of punctuation and rhythm, examining grammatical words and conjunctions, "fillers" that are unacceptable (as such) in the language and which we have to learn to read at their true level of meaning.[26]

The Principle of Precision (Competing Signs)

The idea of an expression that is fully significant is inseparable from the presupposition that this expression is absolutely precise. Sensitive to variations in form but rejecting a priori any hint of abitrariness, the rabbis attacked the theory of a subjective, "literary" mode of writing. To explain these aleatory elements, they developed a highly complex and extremely refined system of reading that connects morphology, syntax, and semantics. Malbim's compilation is only one example of this: "And anyone who believes in the holiness of our Torah and in the splendor of its language will understand that this kind of [variation in] expression could in no case result from chance or the author's whim. . . . Our Sages have noted each of these contexts and studied the formulation, and they have ruled on them."[27]

Each statement is clear, exact, with no penumbra of uncertainty. This principle of precision would at first seem to preclude certain effects of sense radiating in different directions—such as connotation and ambiguity. However, the rule of absolute character of the sense is not restrictive but rather cumulative and totalizing. In the connotative order, each term is presumed to recapitulate within itself all the correspondences that traverse it, all the harmonics it evokes.

In the order of ambiguity, ambivalence is not resolved but integrated into the meaning: competing interpretations are not only considered equivalent, but equally and simultaneously authenticated. Thus meaning is multiplied and actualized in readings that are diverse but complementary rather than mutually exclusive.

"And so, in the case of each deviant expression, our Sages have explained the *double* intention of the text, for the Torah has not arbitrarily chosen an ambiguous form of expression."[28]

Perfection of meaning thus seems to be paradoxically defined by the undifferentiated, which broadens its scope.

THE MOTIVATION OF LANGUAGE
(EXPRESSION/CONTENT)

Ultimately, the key to traditional interpretation lies in the conviction that biblical language is motivated at all levels; as Word, it is called on to found and speak the world. It derives Adam from *adamah* (the earth) and *ishah* (woman) from *ish* (man). Through it, the first man gives a name to all creatures, whose identity he discerns.

Dictated by God (to Moses), the Torah conforms to the world He created. It is homologous with the real—a sort of vast ideogram.[29] Thus, by cultural and metaphysical choice, there is a homonymy among diverse signifying sets, from the real to the sign. This homology is reproduced, within language, in a reciprocal symbolization linking the level of expression and the level of content.

In this respect, it is striking that exegetical logic is based on a formal as well as a conceptual deduction, lexical and syntagmatic contiguity serving as an argument just as much as logical connection or the paradigmatic sequence of equivalences in sense.

Hence one finds in the Kabbalah,[30] treated as equally evident in the effort to classify biblical terms according to the ten cosmic "spheres" of spiritual experience, a syntagmatic foundation (the appearance of terms belonging to the same class in the same verse); lexical associations, *berkhah-berekhah* (benediction-reservoir); and a thematic paradigm based on analogy, *be'er-yam-berekhah* (well-sea-reservoir).

The traditional mentality is not at all bothered by these continual movements from a signifying sequence to a signified sequence. For this mentality, it is neither possible nor desirable to make such a distinction: it is the imbrication of systems that guarantees the coherence of the universe as principle of faith. The concrete and the abstract, form and content, truth and reality, can be included within each other and proceed from the same unity: it is this philosophical choice of unity, echoed at every level of belief, that organizes the whole of exegetical thought.

This acknowledged coherence linking language and thought seems to make all the more legitimate a properly linguistic approach, as distinct from regular conceptual studies, which would seek to recover, starting from the morphological level itself, the hidden organization of sense. In midrashic, talmudic, and kabbalistic commentary we will follow the development not of an idea but of a term, attempting to reconstruct on this basis the inverted pyramid of interpretations.

This approach, which is purely synchronic, will authorize recourse to chronologically disparate sources: neither the Talmud nor the Midrash is a monolithic unity—not to mention the Zohar, concerning which there is so much disagreement about the date of its first conception. Moreover, traditional hermeneutic coherence assimilates and transcends the possible variations over the centuries, by means of a commentary that always comes back to recultivate the same furrows, in spite of profound changes.

Taking into account the principle of plenitude mentioned earlier, we have situated the question at its most sensitive point: at a level of language that in Western experience is felt to be essentially grammatical or functional.

We will limit our study to the analysis of the semantic status granted to (biblical) "grammatical words" by commentary in the Midrash and certain kabbalistic texts, and more specifically to the deictic category of demonstratives. The latter constitute a set of terms whose reference is variable and which are thus impossible to pin down semantically. A punctual signification[31] determined by context is attributed to them in each particular occurrence, and this signification is displaced by the following one.

The phenomena of *deixis* seem in fact to focus within themselves the entire problematics of sense in the Mosaic heritage: as "empty" elements of the vocabulary, deictics raise questions in a text that claims "plenitude." But at the same time they are emblematic, in a way, of the general semantic functioning of the Torah, in that they are reactualized in each context; permanent *and* changeable, in language they symbolize the opening of sense onto the real, onto a *present* word to be reformulated. It is on this lack, this call for explanation, this "lapsus" of expression, that the richest truths will be established.

Before defining commentary's particular sensitivity to relational terms in the Torah, if there are grounds for doing so, let us postulate the interest of focusing attention on the point where we find best articulated the inversion of the two linguistics (conventional and logical), which constitute two different conceptions of language.

Given the particular corpus of demonstratives (*zeh, zot*), we will analyze the forms and stages of their semantic investment by commentary in a progressive phenomenon of hypostasis with complex modalities.

Starting out from the traditional registers of interpretation, we will distinguish in this process four main methodological orientations, organized around the central concept of equivalence as philosophy and as praxis. The first two, Peshat and Sod, are at the opposite extremes of the hermeneutic chain and establish exegesis on constant and determinate bases. They are centered respectively on the sense of the demonstrative in language and on the conventional interpretation of anagogy.

The other two—which correspond to the intermediate modalities of Remez and Derash[32]—seek instead to bring out the range of possible references, whose polyvalence they respect. They are based both on a system of combination internal to the text, with its play and reversals, and on an infinite number of existential situations that allow the actualization of its message.

The set of techniques of reading, which are convergent and all included within the same ideological coherence, Peshat, Remez, Derash, and Sod (literal, allusive, parabolic, and anagogic readings), constitutes the *PaRDeS* or Garden of Knowledge, the PaRaDiSe of wisdom.

Not the least surprising outcome of this study will be the discovery of a unified organic whole that brings together disparate hermeneutic categories and contradictory functions: caught between dynamism and completion, exegesis watches over unforeseeable mutations, making chance responses conform to the deep code of its truth. It interweaves the diverse layers of interpretation into a calculated system with inexhaustible resources.

Thus decoding has no true autonomy at either level, even literal and immediate. The simplest reading evokes secret harmonics, and even its obviousness is already caught up in the net of a cultural choice: the Hebrew Bible, as a text, is not the Greek Septuagint or the Latin Vulgate of the Christians.

This last remark may allow us to indicate one of the main lines of our study: the definition, within a privileged ideological unity that is both structured and open, of the articulation between a meaning and a culture that bears it, the encounter between a language and a worldview. My analysis will seek to circumvent this junction point, which is the object of semantics and still remains very mysterious, to the extent that one can hope to do so: that is, by choosing a precise example (demonstratives) and a systematic approach.

What emerges from this investigation is the compatibility, at every level, of exegetical approaches that are contrary to each other (or seem so to the West), blending the living with the absolute, metamorphoses of sense with the permanence of truth. These exegetical approaches reflect the intersection of curved and straight lines, the experience of the limit that religious consciousness calls *kedushah,* "sanctification," and whose fulcrum language designates by the demonstrative *zeh:* "this" or "that" which is revealed to me *through this world.*

The reader has no doubt recognized underlying this methodological transposition, and *redefined in Hebrew terms,* the metaphysical dialectic of incarnation, understood as the inscription of the spiritual in matter.

1

The Sense of the Demonstrative

Following the trail blazed by logic and philosophy, modern linguistics raises the question of the relationship between language and reality through the problematics of reference. Whatever vocabulary is adopted for this purpose, the progression from the word[1] to the object it represents passes through the detour of the *sense*: "The reference of an expression is the object named or denoted by it. We must distinguish this object from the sense of the expression. . . . The sense of a sign, Frege says, contains the 'mode of presentation' whereby the sign gives us its reference."[2]

Perhaps symbolically, this mediate structure is in accord with the perspective and scope of the present study. I have in fact taken as my primary task the analysis, on the basis of the example of the Hebrew demonstrative *zeh*, of the manipulations of meaning by which traditional exegesis arrives at the specific references elucidated in its commentary.

The case of the demonstrative provides a particularly fertile field of study because it belongs to a class of terms with variable reference—deictics—where what is at *stake* is precisely this dialectic of the determinate and the indeterminate, of an already formed meaning and a designation that has always to be made again. We will see that in this ambivalence the dialectical principle of all Jewish hermeneutics is crystallized, polarized at its source between the Written Law and the Oral Law, between fixity and flexibility.

Thus by starting out from a grasp on the points of contact

between the data of a linguistic or philosophical description and the extent to which rabbinical commentary respects or transgresses its presuppositions, we can reconstruct a thematics and the rules of interpretation peculiar to exegesis. The latter oscillates between the laws of writing and the imperatives of truth, between the a priori conditions of a conventional meaning and the (actual) plurivalence of possible readings.

THE LINGUISTIC POINT OF VIEW

Deictics[3] constitute one of the essential points in a theory of reference. They are defined as mobile signs, having a sense in the language but designating in each instance of use a new reference, which is situated with respect to the interlocutors. In this respect, deictics could be seen as forming a class of parameters of the real in language, and they are placed at the point of articulation between the existential and the linguistic.

Chiefly, this class of signs includes personal pronouns, adverbs of place and time, demonstratives, certain articles, and more generally all grammatical elements that presuppose a reference to the concrete situation of discourse in which they are uttered: thus "I" identifies—differently each time—the speaker; "this," his or her immediate environment; "here" and "now," the spatiotemporal context of utterance.

"It is easily seen that all these words can be defined in terms of the phrase 'this token.' The word 'I,' for instance, means the same as 'the person who utters this token'; 'now' means the same as 'the time at which this token is uttered'; 'this table' means the same as 'the table pointed to by a gesture accompanying this token.'"[4]

The "token" is the particular utterance indicating a single, current reference. It is distinguished from the generic expression or "type," whose still undifferentiated meaning is abstracted from any particular actualization.

In these definitions of the deictic act of reference we note a double characteristic of unity and mobility: "language . . . [institutes] a unique but mobile sign, I, which can be assumed by each speaker on the condition that he refers each time only to the instance of his own discourse."[5]

The shifter is thus simultaneously undefined, open to any kind of determination whatever—in the contemporary sense of the "open work"—and specific with regard to each punctual reference it establishes. This double characteristic is inscribed in the signified of the sign, which by definition bears the mark of this void.

The demonstrative, when it is deictic, takes on this ambivalence. Through its indexical function, it delimits the relation of human beings to their environment, their first inquiry into the world. If it permits univocal determinations pointing precisely toward "this" or "that," at the same time it preserves the referential "mobility" peculiar to *deixis,* which redefines the object every time it designates it.

On these grounds, the demonstrative has often been considered, especially by logicians, as the archetype of *deixis,* a fundamental sign from which all others could be derived: "All 'egocentric words'[6] can be defined in terms of 'this.' Thus 'I' means 'The biography to which this belongs'; 'here' means 'The place of this'; 'now' means 'The time of this'; and so on. We may therefore confine our inquiry to 'this.'"[7]

We know, however, that these sets only partially intersect, since the class of demonstratives includes both deictics and anaphorics.[8] The anaphoric demonstrative is a term referring back to what has already been said or seen in a preceding context (of a statement or utterance); it can be integrated into the existential experience of interlocutors only in a deferred manner, through the memory of what is already known.

When it has a deictic value, that is, when it designates an object present in the context of utterance, the demonstrative synthesizes two semantic modalities that are also two aspects of knowledge. The speaker can call the addressee's attention to the nature (qualification) or to the place (location) of the object to which he is referring: "Broadly speaking, there are two ways in which we can identify an object by means of a referring expression: first, by informing the addressee where it is (i.e., by locating it for him); second, by telling him what it is like, what properties it has or what class of objects it belongs to (i.e., by describing it for him)."[9]

With this distinction, which Lyons seems to consider universal in the ontogenesis of languages, the demonstrative is fully established as a linguistic category, a general category of language and philosophy that is just as fundamental as that of the subject or the predicate. Its semantic possibilities are immense, its polarizations subtle and already ambiguous.

Thus the role it plays in grammatical and philological studies of the Bible will not surprise us. In our analysis, these studies will be presented from the exegetical point of view, which filters the results in accord with its own mode of reading.

THE PHILOLOGICAL POINT OF VIEW

The semantic arrangement we have proposed, insofar as it seems to cover the whole field of natural languages, allows us to resolve an immediate problem encountered by any study of demonstratives in the Bible: the problem of the insertion of a heterogeneous category—developed on the basis of Western thought—into a textual whole foreign to the metalanguage applied to it. At the same time we have to acknowledge the possibility of an autonomous categorization, internal to the biblical corpus considered as an idiolect.

A scholar can therefore bring out a designative sense inherent in *zeh* starting from two key contexts in which the value of "ostension"[10] specific to the demonstrative is as it were made explicit and defined: "Now *this* [*zeh*] is how the lampstand was made: it was hammered work of gold, hammered from base to petal. According to the *pattern* [*représentation*] that the Lord had shown Moses, so was the lampstand made" (Num. 8:4).[11]

The second passage is clearer: "Moses went up from the steppes of Moab to Mount Nebo, to the summit of Pisgah, opposite Jericho, and the Lord *showed* him the whole land: Gilead as far as Dan; all Naphtali; the land of Ephraim and Manasseh. . . . And the Lord said to him '*This*' [*zot*] is the land of which I swore to Abraham, Isaac and Jacob, 'I will give it to your offspring.' I have let you see it with your own eyes, but you shall not cross there" (Deut. 34:1–4). Thus is posited a general sense of *presentation* (concrete representation) coherent with the internal logic of the text.

On the basis of examples of this kind, with the theoretical support of a "natural" category of the demonstrative and by means of an exhaustive inventory of its uses in the Bible, classical philology infers the existence of an autonomous class. We will study this class in the exemplary case of the deictic pronoun *zeh*, which is simultaneously a pronoun, an adjective, and an adverb, and which is marked in dictionaries and grammars of biblical Hebrew by a high degree of syntactical and semantic polyvalence.[12]

The famous Gesenius grammar,[13] still an authoritative reference, distinguishes the following uses of the word: (a) adjective or demonstrative pronoun; (b) relative pronoun; (c) emphatic adverb in certain phrases (spatiotemporal indications, interrogatives).[14]

In its demonstrative use, the pronoun-adjective *zeh* (feminine *zot, zou*,[15] plural *eleh*) competes with the definite article *Ha*, on the one hand, and the third-person personal pronoun *hu* (feminine *hi*), on the other. This classification remains valid today and is echoed in recent studies on biblical language.[16] The same distinctions, with a few slight differences, reappear in dictionaries of ancient Hebrew or Chaldean such as Harkavi's[17] and in etymological dictionaries of modern Hebrew,[18] classical reference works concerning all strata of the language. They acknowledge that *zeh* can have the value of (1) a pronoun or demonstrative adjective; (2) a relative pronoun (or "relational term"); (3) an adverb of time or place (with the meaning "already" when it precedes a temporal unit); and (4) a means of emphasis in interrogative phrases (reinforcing an interrogative pronoun).

The presentation in Ben-Yehuda's dictionary alone departs somewhat from this schema,[19] in that it stresses a syntactical point of view and defines rules of usage for each grammatical category. For instance, it distinguishes the pronoun from the adjective in relation to word order, and so on. This unusual point of view allows us to deal with another problem, which has to do with the previously mentioned opposition[20] between *deixis* and anaphora. Whereas most dictionaries—if they raise the question at all—distinguish the deictic form *zeh* (this one) from the anaphoric *hu* (that one),[21] Ben-Yehuda's relocates this distinction within the usage modalities of the demonstrative *zeh* itself: in the singular and in the feminine, *zeh* can take the place of the neuter, as an anaphoric, to refer to "what we have already mentioned." These divergences indicate the risks run by a study of deictic phenomena—that is, phenomena linked to the process of utterance—in a "dead" language such as ancient Hebrew.

Examples of these diverse forms occur in the Bible as if there were no significant difference between them; the demonstrative *zeh* occupies a space intermediate between the article *Ha* and the demonstrative *hu*, which replace it without difficulty in apparently equivalent phrases. The distinction between pure and anaphoric deictics becomes particularly thorny:

> The Lord your God commands you *this day (zeh)*.
> (Deut. 26:16)

> You go free on *this day*, in the month of Abib (*Ha*).
> (Exod. 13:4)

And again:

> On *that very day* they entered the wilderness (*zeh*).
> (Exod. 19:1)

> You shall explain to your son on *that day (hu)*.
> (Exod. 13:8)

One finds the same triad used to refer to "the land":

> I will give *this land* to your offspring (*zot*).
> (Gen. 12:7, 24:7)

Then, when the Lord has given us *this land (Ha)*.
> (Josh. 2:14)

> To bring them out of *that land* (*hi*, the feminine of *hu*).
> (Exod. 3:8)

On the strictly linguistic level, the variety of formulations does not permit any univocal characterization.

There is an additional difficulty connected with the special status of biblical narrative; unfolding a series of existential situations that form a context of utterance, this narrative has at the same time the value of a ritual text that is cut off from any reference to experience, and whose "objects of discourse" can be grasped only as abstract signs. This point of view might seem clearly to strengthen the totally contextualized anaphoric valence of the demonstrative in the Bible: problematizing the notion of reference, it makes ambiguous the deictic functioning attached to it.

In a monograph on biblical *deixis*, the linguist K. Ehlich[22] has made an interesting attempt to resolve the problem by treating as deictic in character all uses of *zeh* in discourse, including those that seem to be anaphoric and centered on the utterance. This "deicticization" of all occurrences of *zeh* reserves for the pronoun *hu* descriptions in the third person and descriptions of distance.

Ehlich's argument is based on a redefinition of the concepts.[23] To ensure the hegemony of *zeh* as a deictic demonstrative, he is led first of all to consider the cases in which it is used in direct discourse, which represent almost 70 percent of the total of its occurrences in the Bible, and then to extend what he calls "the deictic space" to the remaining cases. In this way he forges the notion of the "*deixis* of discourse," which attributes to discursive acts themselves the value of deictic objects, both as illocutionary acts and as propositions. Similarly, he resolves the paradox of "textual *deixis*" by analyzing it in terms of internal reference: the demonstrative makes it possible to *designate* a *citation* inserted into the space of discourse.

We have mentioned Ehlich's argument because of its original effort to isolate *zeh* as a demonstrative category that is specifically and wholly deictic, and which allows us to separate it radically from the usage of the anaphoric *hu*: "The two classes of expressions (*hu* and *zeh*) serve two different purposes in speech acts. I arrive at definitions of *deixis* and anaphor, respectively, which read as follows:

- The deictic procedure is a linguistic means to achieve the focusing of the hearer's attention toward a specific item that is part of the respective deictic space.
- This deictic procedure is performed by means of deictic expressions (*zeh*).
- The anaphoric procedure is a linguistic means to make the hearer continue (sustain) a previously established focus toward a specific item to which he had oriented his attention before.
- The anaphoric procedure is performed by means of anaphoric expressions (*hu*).[24]

This reading allows us to range all *zeh*'s references under the rubric of *deixis* and to adopt a single order of criteria. This reading also responds to the objection regarding the "distance" of the biblical text with respect to any existential actualization. The notion of a *deixis* of discourse becomes applicable to "objects" of reference belonging to the order of the sign as well as to that of reality. The door thus remains open to a referential projection of a thematic sort[25] that would note within the demonstrative function a typical trait of ambivalence or of open determination.

The Exegetical Point of View

When linguistic functioning is taken into account by traditional exegesis, it is made dependent on a conventional evaluation that reserves the right to recognize or invalidate its premises. Commentary's linguistic sensibility is asserted but at the same time regulated in accord with an implicit cultural code. Its a priori assumption, in Malbim's opinion,[26] is a policy of nonintervention in cases in which the text seems to be determined strictly by the requirements of the expression (grammatical, stylistic, or logical in nature): "When the word is in accord with the rules of the language, there is no reason to resort to interpretation."[27] This point of view is usually challenged to allow more arbitrariness in exegetical intervention. It remains valuable especially on the hermeneutic level of Peshat, that is, the literal or immediate comprehension of biblical narrative.

Whatever the definition adopted—and definitions are often problematic and vary from one commentator to another—this *zero degree* of reading and its exegetical apparatus are always subordinated to the presuppositions of language. However, these presuppositions are themselves not easy to define, and ultimately they are related to a larger ideology that partially determines them. The three other levels of exegesis, which are illustrated by all forms of Midrash,[28] claim to differing degrees this independent inspiration that is more or less directly connected with the text's expression.

We may observe, in fact, a certain autonomy of the hermeneutic classification with respect to the philologists' taxonomy. Whatever the pertinence of these divisions borrowed from Indo-European linguistics, Midrash retains only the distinctive traits that are compatible with its exegetical apparatus and that serve its ideology. Perhaps we should speak here of "conditions of use" of a specific type, of a sort of "ideologics" of language (modeled on its "pragmatics") corresponding to precise external norms.

In that case, the reevaluation of purely grammatical categories does not directly affect the system of signification constructed by traditional commentary. In this way the validity of a categorization in language would be maintained, but by recognizing stable methodological principles, it would avoid the danger of arbitrary classification. While classical philology believed it was justified, on the basis of a meticulous, detailed examination of the text, in delimiting a demonstrative group in biblical Hebrew, this theoretical or methodological detour would not be necessary for the elucidation of the corresponding exegetical paradigm.

The first principle of commentary is that of total meaningfulness: the slightest deviation, the slightest uncertainty or impropriety in expression is delved into, "turned over," by exegesis.[29] In this respect, it is especially the redundancies that seem "scandalous" and therefore significant. For the rabbis, there is no possible *neutralization* of terms by displacing the norm that would lead, as in diachronic linguistics, to an erosion of the categories and to their restructuring.

The threshold of sensitivity to these phenomena is therefore very low. That is why traditional commentary puts on the list of rhetorical puzzles to be explained several of the stylistic effects mentioned by dictionaries and grammars, such as an emphatic use of *zeh* (in interrogatives) or its use as an adverbial support (in temporal expressions). Thus in Esau's exclamation "Why do I need my birthright *then*?" (Gen. 25:32), where *zeh* is generally translated as an emphatic "then" or "thus" (cf. Harkavi's translation), the Midrash condemns the presence of the demonstrative as a redundancy and assumes the task of "normalizing" the usage by an appropriate thematic development.[30]

In the same way, according to the rhetorical level adopted, commentary chooses to intervene or not to intervene to account for general presentational or concluding turns of phrase that add no direct *information* regarding the subject but facilitate reading and allow the coherence of the discussion to be more easily followed. Thus Rabbi Yoshiah draws a lesson from expressions of the type "such is the law of jealousy" or "such is the law of the ascetic," which have a supererogatory character, whereas Rabbi Yonathan asserts regarding the same texts that these are pure formulas of conclusion, traditional figures of style that offer no foothold (or pretext) for interpretation.[31]

The second important characteristic of exegetical procedure is a more pronounced taste for linguistic phenomena that promote semanticization: rabbinical philology passes through morphology and syntax to draw from them the "substantial marrow" of a meaning. The recognized grammatical assumptions are thus the ones that concern or condition the semantic value of the pronoun, while other fundamental divisions are not maintained or noted in the Midrash.

We have discovered no regularity (even hidden or indirect, at any level in the distribution of commentaries) that is founded on a possible distinction between the pronoun and the adjective. Similarly, the use of *zeh* as a relative pronoun is not exploited by traditional commentary. On the other hand, the distinction between genders is retained and even leads to a complete thematic cycle. We know that this distinction is not complete in Hebrew, in that it differentiates the masculine from the feminine, but melds the feminine with the neuter. The Talmud takes advantage of this ambiguity. The morpheme *zot* is taken as feminine or as neuter according to the requirements of the interpretation, and sometimes without regard to an immediate reading: "Here is how (*bezot;* literally, with this) Aaron entered the sanctuary: with a bull of the herd for a sin offering and a ram for a burnt offering" (Lev. 16:3). The Gemara asks: Is *zot* a neuter here (in which case the text is grammatically correct: "Here is how [= like this] Aaron entered the sanctuary"), or should it be understood as feminine, which would violate the rule of agreement in gender: "With 'this' [feminine] Aaron entered the sanctuary: with a bull . . . and a ram [masculine]." On the basis of this second hypothesis, which is attractive because of its thematic potential in spite of the fact that it is less probable logically, the Talmud is led to propose an unusual interpretation that explains this irregularity.[32]

As for number, which is indicated in the language by a change in the radical, it corresponds to so clear a lexical (and thematic) transformation that we have preferred to exclude it from our area of investigation in spite of its use in Midrash.[33]

It remains to examine what happens in exegesis to the double opposition that structures the analysis of *zeh,* the one opposing the use of *zeh* to the conditions for using the article (*ha*) and the other opposing the use of *zeh* to those for using the anaphoric demonstrative (*hu*). Commentary carefully examines these distinctions, which compel it, on the basis of a principle of precision or economy of language, to account for the particular *choice* of each expression. Any ambivalence raises questions by its very possibility, and the neighboring permutations of the demonstrative constitute in themselves a call for interpretation.

We know that in Hebrew the definite article (*ha*) has a demonstrative value that makes it compete in certain contexts with the demonstrative adjective proper. For exegesis, it there-fore provokes a justificatory development. We find these phil-osophical questions explicitly formulated in the most recent commentators, who are generally less allusive in their exposi-tion of the argument.

Thus *Torah Or*[34] notes an occasional redundancy in the use of *zeh*, in comparison to other contexts in which the definite ar-ticle seems to suffice for designation: "Thus we note numerous passages in which the demonstrative *zeh* (*zot*) seems superflu-ous: for example, in the verse 'The Lord your God commands you *this* day today [*hayom hazeh*, instead of *hayom*, "today"]' (Deut. 26:16). . . . The word *zeh* is redundant here since we find the same construction in other contexts where it does not occur; for instance, in 'You go free today (*hayom*) in the month of Abib' (Exod. 13:4)."[35]

In this ambivalence, the demonstrative seems to be marked with respect to the neuter form represented by the normal use of the article. It is thus specialized in a determination of unique-ness, whose connotations in exegesis rapidly take on the value of a specific trait.[36]

The second opposition, which is internal to the category of the demonstrative, brings out the criterion of proximity. Exe-gesis is sensitive to this opposition, which is produced lexically in biblical language and based, as in Latin, on a determination of place and person. Exegesis recognizes as the characteristic semantic function of *zeh* the designation of a nearby, visible object in the concrete universe which is connected with the (first-person) speaking subject: "this" in opposition to the pro-noun/adjective *hahu*, "that," which is derived from *hu* (he, him, the third-person personal pronoun), which designates a distant object disconnected from the speaking subject.

As *Torah Or* puts it,

Thus [we encounter the expressions] "On that day (*zeh*) all the fountains of the great deep burst apart . . ." (Gen. 7:11); "On this very day (*hahu*), they entered the wilderness of Sinai" (Exod. 19:1); "On this day (*hahu*) the Lord made a covenant with Abram" (Gen. 15:18); "And you shall explain to your son on that day (*hahu*)" (Exod. 13:8). What is the difference between *hazeh* and *hahu*? . . . It resides in the fact that the demonstrative *hahu* designates an object distant from us, whereas *zeh* indicates a nearby object. . . . And thus, each time *zeh* is used to refer to a distant thing, our sages have drawn a lesson from this.[37]

Here we see once again the awareness and noting down of several competing formulations, the refusal to amalgamate them, and the regulative choice of a necessary hierarchy.

As a demonstration of exegetical functioning, *Torah Or* reports the following commentary:

And here is how Rashi[38] explains, following the Midrash, Exodus 19:1: "On this very day (*zeh*) they entered the wilderness of Sinai": the text should have said: "on that very day" [since it is a narrative in the past]; why do we find the expression "this day" [in the present]? So that the words of the Torah might be as new to you as if they had just been transmitted to you *today*. In the same way, Rashi says about the verse "The Lord your God commands you this day" (Deut. 26:16), let His commandments be each day as if they were new to you.[39]

This last distinction brings us back to the fundamental opposition between *deixis* and anaphora. If, through the interpretation of the Midrash, it is possible to recognize the demonstrative's deictic status, this results less from its relation to the present of utterance than from its role as a semantic signal. Traditional commentary experiences the presence of *zeh* as marking *immediacy*, without being concerned to delve into its linguistic structuring. The opposition between the utterance and the act of uttering seems to be neutralized here in favor of a general thematics that focuses, in the act of reference, only on the specific signifieds that it puts into play.

THE ANALYSIS OF SENSE

This double task of elucidation, deciding between replacement by the article or replacement by the anaphoric pronoun, ends up demonstrating, through a series of privileged distinctive traits, what the fundamental sense of the demonstrative represented for exegesis. These traits reconstruct a clearly outlined, homogeneous semantic whole. Beneath the individual cases and disseminated explanations, a specific hermeneutic approach is constituted, which is essentially connected with the occurrence of the demonstrative as such, independently from any contextual reference.

We will present here an overall classification of these (sense-centered) commentaries, that is, those that are based primarily on the autonomous *sense of the demonstrative in the linguistic system*. Exegesis tends here in fact to make autonomous the semantic indications that the demonstrative sense presupposes, at the expense of those provided by its reference in context.[40]

DOUBLE SEMANTIC STRUCTURING

Zeh/Ha: The Pseudoemphatic Use of Zeh

In contrast with the use of the definite article, which establishes an existential presupposition, the presence of the demonstrative adds to that determination a mark of specificity and uniqueness: "this," precisely "this" and not something else. In exegesis, this modality governs quantity as well as quality: the appearance of *zeh* allows commentary to discern the extent of the designation, in extension (restriction: exclusively "this") and in comprehension (specification: exactly "this").

Thus the Talmud examines the meaning of the commandment transmitted by Moses to read "this Torah" (*hazoth*) before all Israel once every seven years (Deut. 31:11). The expression "this Torah" must be understood here as referring to the fifth scroll of the Pentateuch, *stricto sensu*, that is, exclusively the one that contains the prescribed command (restriction), or as referring to the *original text* of the Torah, "this Torah" exactly, that is, in its Hebraic version (specification).[41]

In the following examples, the presence of the demonstrative is questioned because of its apparent redundancy, and exploited in the sense of *restriction*:

Until the fourteenth day of this very month (*hazeh*).
(Exod. 12:6)

The Gemara immediately reacts:

Hazeh lamah li? Why "this very month" instead of "this month," which is sufficiently explicit? It is in order to *exclude* the case of Pesah Sheni.

(*Pesahim* 96a)[42]

In this very jubilee year [*hazoth*].
(Lev. 25:13)

In this year: this very one [the jubilee year, strictly speaking] automatically frees the slaves, whereas the seventh year [= the year of *Shemita*] does not free them.

(*Sifra* 108d)[43]

And on the fifteenth day of this month (*hazeh*), it will be the Feast of Unleavened Bread.

(Lev. 23:6)

Sifra connects the presence of the word *zeh* with the limitation of the precept of the *matzoh* (unleavened bread) to the Passover feast alone (whereas a logical argument could be made for extending the obligation to the feast of the Tabernacles): "The inference is based on *zeh*: *This very day* includes the obligation to eat *matza*, but not the feast of the Tabernacles" (*Sifra* 100d).

Similarly:

They shall eat the flesh that same night (*Hazeh*).
(Exod. 12:8)

Rabbi Akiva teaches: *This* very night, to the exclusion of any other night.

(*Berakhoth* 9a)

Or again:

If an ox gores a minor, male or female, the owner shall be dealt with according to this very law.

(Exod. 21:31)

This very law: the appearance of the term *zeh* allows us to *exclude* four other cases of condemnation.

(*Bava Kamma* 33a)

In a second series, the commentary *clarifies the nature* of the object (conceptual or real) to which *zeh* refers:

> This (*zot*) shall be the ritual for a leper at the time that he is to be cleansed.
>
> (Lev. 14:2)

> This shall be: this shall be precisely the ritual [to be followed scrupulously].
>
> (*Menahoth* 5a)

Similarly, concerning the adulterous woman:

> The priest shall carry out all this (*zot*) ritual with her.
>
> (Num. 5:30)

> This ritual in every respect: *precisely* as it is set forth. To teach you that any modification invalidates it.
>
> (*Midrash Rabbah*, Num. 9:27)

Or again:

> Here (*bezoth*) is how Aaron shall enter the shrine.
>
> (Lev. 16:3)

> The Holy One, blessed-be-He, said to Moses: Aaron may enter the sanctuary at any time, on the condition that he observe the rules of worship according to the *order* of the prescribed rites.
>
> (*Midrash Rabbah*, Lev. 21:7)

Along with these examples defining a legal or ritual mode of conduct,[44] we find a value of specifying the object as such, in a use similar to that of the English "itself," as in "the thing itself":

> This (*zeh*) shall be a sacred anointing oil.
>
> (Exod. 30:31)

> The oil made by Moses . . . is preserved for future times.
>
> (*Keritoth* 5a–b)

The expression "sacred anointing oil" appears several times in the passage unaccompanied by *zeh*, except in this verse where the text extends the precept to future generations: "This shall be an anointing oil sacred to Me throughout the ages." "This": this very oil, made by Moses, shall be used to anoint the future kings and priests of Israel, and beyond them, the royal Messiah.

Zeh/Hu: The Deictic Use of Zeh

In opposition to *hu*, the demonstrative of distance, *zeh* defines a proximity to the speaking subject, which is the proximity of *deixis* proper. For exegesis, this semantic trait is fundamental in that it specifies *zeh* as a demonstrative of objects "that can be pointed to with the finger" and are situated in the speaker's immediate surroundings.

> A man marries a woman and cohabits with her. Then he takes an aversion to her and makes up charges against her and defames her, saying, "I married this woman (*hazoth*); but when I approached her, I found that she was not a virgin."
>
> (Deut. 22:13)[45]
>
> *This* woman: we learn thereby that he accuses her only in her presence.
>
> (*Sifré*, Pent. 268 L3)[46]

The use of *zeh*, in contrast with *hu*, has as its primary function to integrate the object into the immediacy of discourse, bringing it into the visual field of communication. "*That* woman" would be the one spoken of; and "*this* woman" is the one present at the moment of utterance, directly accused by her detractor.

Similarly:

> This son of ours (*zeh*) is disloyal and defiant.
>
> (Deut. 21:20)
>
> One can infer from this formulation that if one of the parents is *blind*, the son does not fall within the judicial category of "disloyal and defiant son."
>
> (*Sanhedrin* 71a)

The *Torah Temima*[47] attributes this position to a linguistic sensitivity:

> We find explained in the Gemara of *Pesahim* (116b) the basis of this interpretation; in fact, the text should have said: "Our son"; the presence of *zeh* adds here an idea of concrete designation ('pointing with the finger'): "this son that we all *see*."[48]

> When the time came for her to give birth, there were twins in her womb! While she was in labor, one of them put out his hand,

and the midwife tied a crimson thread on that hand, to signify: This one (*zeh*) was born first.

(Gen. 38:27–28)

This one was born first: we infer from this that the midwife is qualified to identify the eldest child as such.

(*Yerushalmi, Kidushin* 4, 2)

The validity of her testimony is supported by the use of the deictic *zeh*: the person who was so close to the child to be born is thereby authorized to attest to his right as firstborn.

Other commentators stress a proximity in time: "O Lord, why did You bring harm upon this people (*hazeh*)?" (Exod. 5:22):

Moses addressed the Holy One, blessed-be-He in these terms: I have taken the book of Genesis and I have read it, I have seen the misdeeds of the generation of the flood, and their condemnation by the attribute of Judgment, and the misconduct of the generations of Babel and Sodom, and their condemnation by the attribute of Judgment. What has *this people* done, to be enslaved more than all the previous generations?

(*Midrash Rabbah* 5, 22)

This explanation is based on the use here of *zeh*, which authorizes by its "coefficient of presentness" the rereading of "people" as "generation."

AUTONOMIZATION

These few examples illustrate the recognition and exploitation by hermeneutics of a specific sense inherent in the demonstrative. The semantic traits stressed, which coincide more or less with the fundamental categories of the corresponding linguistic paradigm, could be recapitulated in the following manner: given a present object in the spatiotemporal field of the interlocutors, *zeh* designates a relation of proximity between the speaker and this object—which is assumed to be defined with respect to quantity and/or quality.

Up to this point, commentary seems to have been concerned with clarifying only an insufficiently precise or poorly defined relation between determinants and what is determined. It also happens, and most often, that Midrash goes beyond this function of making explicit to upset the equilibrium of the relations of determination. Indeed, if we consider that the meaning of the demonstrative presents in language the instructions for use necessary to locate its reference in the discourse, we will recognize in numerous commentaries a phenomenon of overdetermination that endows these purely grammatical instructions with a semantic value of their own.[49]

In this way a sort of thematic autonomy emerges from the demonstrative which produces its own information—like any other sort of grammatical category—beyond the mere designation of the referential relation it governs. At the same time, the deictic process is gradually blocked. This mechanism becomes apparent in the examples where the presence of *zeh*, experienced as inadequate, calls for a semantic normalization by commentary. In fact, in case of conflict between the a priori givens of the sense and the imperatives of the context, *the former prevail*.

This autonomization is exercised in a double register, syntactical (producing an effect of "signalization") or semantic (producing an effect of "thematization").

a) In the first case, which usually corresponds to redundant formulations of a rhetorical sort, the cataphoric[50] construction of presentation is unsatisfactory for exegesis, which breaks this unacceptable *syntactical* structure by making the demonstrative an *operator* of signification with a floating articulation. Its mere presence signals a sememe of an adverbial type, which is attached to one or another of the elements of the context, without a direct referential relation. This sememe is generally that of "restriction" or "specificity" brought out by the opposition between the demonstrative and the article.

b) *Semantic* autonomization draws from the demonstrative its own *qualifying* value that allows the overdetermination of the referential object. It is as if, in the spirit of Midrash, the essential aspect of the description of the object were guaranteed as soon as it was designated, based on definitional traits that seem to contain potentially a sort of identity card, the vacant schema of any future reference.

This form of "reduction" appears in cases of theoretical incompatibility between the presence of *zeh* and the nature of the object referred to. Commentary is then led to replace this incongruous *present* reference by a substitute reference more appropriate to the potential semantic value of the demonstrative sense, and which proves to be determinant.

This referential thematization uses qualifying sememes such as "near" or "concrete," which correspond to the semantic specialization of *zeh* as a deictic.[51]

Signalization

We have seen that the demonstrative, in contrast with the article, performed the function of a means of clarification, specifying or restricting the scope of the point of view on the object. In a second phase, this indicative value associated with *zeh* becomes syntactically autonomous and transforms the demonstrative into a *signal* of meaning, a sort of quantifier or marker of "modality." This function is then applied to any of the elements of the context, and no longer to the specific reference in view, the immediate relation of determination no longer being necessary, as if the demonstrative were free of its articulation in the sentence. This shift is generally made possible by juxtaposing *zeh* with a semantically indefinite term, and by its place at the beginning of a paragraph, thus forming a sort of rhetorical presentation of the subject: "Such (*zot*) are the rituals concerning the woman who bears a child" (Lev. 12:7); "This (*zot*) is the ritual of the sin offering" (Lev. 6:18); "And this (*zot*) is the ritual of the meal offering" (Lev. 6:7); "This (*zot*) is the ritual of the guilt offering" (Lev. 7:1); and so on.

Midrash seems to justify the apparent redundancy connected with this presentation (or more precisely, the redundancy of the word *zeh* within this presentation) by drawing attention to a function of restriction or specification included within this generic expression of presentation. Examples of this are extremely numerous. We will cite only a few of them as illustrations.[52]

This (*zeh*) shall be the nature of the remission [practiced every two years].

(Deut. 15:2)

The seventh year cancels debts, *but not* the fiftieth year [which is the year of the Jubilee].

(*Sifré*, Deut. 173 L1)

This (*zeh*) is what the Lord has commanded concerning the daughters of Zelophehad.

(Num. 36:6)

Such is the commandment: this arrangement is applicable *only* to the desert generation.

(*Taanit* 30b)

Such (*zot*) shall be the ritual for him who has a scaly affection.

(Lev. 14:32)

Such is the ritual: the word "ritual" *includes* the case of a poor leper who has brought the sin offering demanded of the rich man, in order to show us that he has fulfilled his obligation; but then, one might make the complementary argument, and think that the rich leper who had brought the sin offering of a poor one would also be freed of his obligation? It is in order to *exclude* this possibility that the word *zot* appears ['such' will be *precisely* the ritual . . .].

(*Keritoth* 28a)

Finally, on the verse "This shall be the ritual for a leper . . ." (Lev. 14:2): "This shall be: to show you that this ritual is not applicable on an external altar, and must be limited to its altar" (*Sifra* 70c).

In all these examples, the distinctive trait of "restriction" is displaced toward a reference not directly designated by the specific description *zeh* plus substantive. "Such is the ritual" is not the description of the general ritual concerning the leper that is reduced or clarified in its formulation but rather one of the points—this time arbitrarily chosen by the commentary—to which it is applied. In "Such is the commandment" the restriction bears not on the commandment but on the temporal range of its validity.[53]

Moses spoke to the heads of the Israelite tribes, saying: This is what [*zeh hadavar*] the Lord has commanded. If a man makes a vow to the Lord or takes an oath imposing an obligation on himself, he shall not break his pledge.

(Num. 30:2)

This is what the Lord has commanded: the sage can release the wife from her vow, the husband can invalidate it.

(*Nedarim* 78a)[54]

In the same verse, Rabbi Yo'hanan drew from the use of *zeh* the following lesson: "If the sage uses the husband's formula of invalidation, or if the husband uses the sage's formula of release, the procedure is null and void" (*Nedarim* 78a).[55]

This is a striking example of a very clear syntactical (and even syntagmatic) rupture between the occurrence proper of the word *zeh*, in the first sentence of the paragraph cited, and its juridical use based on later verses: "*If a woman* makes a vow to the Lord and assumes an obligation . . . and her husband learns of it and offers no objection on the day he finds out, her vows shall stand and her self-imposed obligations shall stand. But if her husband restrains her on the day that he learns of it, he thereby annuls her vow which was in force or the commitment to which she bound herself" (Num. 30:4, 30:7–9). These verses, which occur in the same context and are interpreted, because of the presence of *zeh*, as rendering the expression more precise, are in fact *separated* from its occurrence by five intervening verses.

A last example of this form:

This then (*vezeh*) shall be the priests' due from the people.

(Deut. 18:3)

Vezeh: Rabbi Hisda taught: "The man who damages the offerings given to the priests, or who consumes them himself [by error], is not required to reimburse them. We infer this from the word *zeh*."

(*Hulin* 130b)

The demonstrative here plays the role of "differential factor" or "specific factor": if the parts devoted to the priests are not delivered to them as such, that is to say, in their original integrity, they move outside the framework of the legislation regarding reimbursement. We note at the same time a further transfer of the designation: the commentary postulates that it is indeed the offering itself that is designated by the demonstrative, not the "regulation" that it seems to introduce into the verse.

Thematization

In opposition to *hu*, the pronoun *zeh* foregrounds the spatio-temporal *immediacy* of the designated object. By a transfer of meaning corollary to the displacement operated by signalization, this relation is now thematized and shifted to the reference itself. The proximity of the object leads, through a shift in determination, to sensing certain of its essential characteristics: being nearby and present, it is therefore experienced as (a) concrete (visualized) and (b) known (recognized). Thus, even more than it situates the object in the temporal context of utterance, *zeh* here allows its integration as a thematic element into the present experience of the interlocutors (or readers).

VISUALIZATION

The Obscurity of Referentialization. Midrash repeatedly intervenes to characterize an imprecise reference of *zeh*. This over-determination is governed by a priori semantic constraints imposed by the sense of the demonstrative and sets forth for reading an object in the universe of discourse that is normally visible and concrete (*"that one points to with one's finger,"* to use the commentator's formula): "You shall explain to your son on that day, 'It is for this reason (*zeh*) that the Lord acted on my behalf when I went free from Egypt'" (Exod. 13:8). In context, the equivocal expression "this reason" will be interpreted in diverse ways. The most classical interpretation, the one preserved in the ritual commemorating the escape from Egypt, is the following: "For this reason: explain to your son only when the *matza* and the bitter herbs are *set before you on the table* [on the evening of Passover]" (*Mekhilta* 66 L, 9).[56]

A second example refers to an episode in the reign of Saul, when the pain of hunger and war drove the people to eat meat "with the blood": "Disperse yourselves among the people, Saul went on, and tell them that every man must bring me his ox or his small animal, slaughter it *here* [or "with this": *bazeh*], and eat it; in this way, you shall not commit against God the sin of eating with the blood" (1 Sam. 14:34): "How should we interpret 'slaughter it here [*bazeh*, whose reference is ambiguous]'? Our Sages tell us: Saul *showed them a knife* [to teach them how long it should be]" (*Midrash Rabbah*, Lev. 25:8).

Redundancy. From the point of view of thematization, redundancy is understood as a discrepancy in meaning. It is not surprising to see the Midrash substitute a concrete and visual representation for a verbal explanation, such as a "surface-level" anaphoric construction might lead us to expect: it appears, in fact, in cases of rhetorical presentation, on which exegesis always stumbles. Three of these examples are collected in a single midrash cited several times—with variants—in midrashic literature and in Gemara:

> Now this (*vezeh*) is how the lampstand was made: it was hammered work of gold, hammered from base to petal. According to the pattern that the Lord had *shown* Moses, so was the lampstand made.
>
> (Num. 8:4–5)
>
> And when you mount the lamps: One finds that Moses experienced more difficulty in making the lampstand than in making any of the other parts of the Tabernacle, until the Holy One, blessed-be-He *showed it to him with his finger.*
>
> (Num. 8:1)
>
> In the same way, God had to show Moses the form of the hooves of clean and unclean animals, as it is written (Lev. 11:2): "Here (*zot*) are the animals you can eat" [whereas the text explains, in an *anaphoric* elaboration: "all that have cleft hooves among the cud-chewing animals"], and, later on, "As for these (*zeh*), you shall not eat them" (Lev. 11:4) [and the text makes this explicit with a list of unclean animals].
>
> (*Midrash Rabbah*, Num. 15:4)

Thus Midrash chooses, on the basis of the presence of *zeh*, to stress a visual and not a verbal mode of teaching. It continues, drawing on the example of the moon and that of the lampstand: "'And *such* is the making of the lampstand, all one piece . . .': to say how difficult it was to make and what pains Moses took in making it" (*Midrash Rabbah*, Num. 15:4).[57] Moreover, the context introduces here, exceptionally, the notion of "representation" (cf. verse 5).

The other examples, whether included in this midrash itself or in variants of it, find in the occurrence of *zeh* sufficient grounds for resorting to the same type of interpretation:

> This very month (*zeh*) shall mark for you the beginning of the months.
>
> (Exod. 12:2)[58]

> This very month: The expression refers to one of the four objects that the Holy One, blessed-be-He showed to Moses (with His finger), because of the difficulties Moses had in carrying out the command concerning them. He showed him how to make the sacred anointing oil, as it is said (Exod. 30:31): "And this shall be the sacred anointing oil" [and the text goes on to make explicit—anaphorically—the laws of anointing]. He showed him how to make the lampstand (Num. 8:4): "This is how to make the lampstand." He pointed out to him the reptiles, as it is said (Lev. 11:29): "Here (*zeh*) are the ones that shall be unclean for you" [and the text continues with a detailed list] and He showed him the moon, as the verse says: "This very month shall mark for you the beginning of the months."
>
> (*Midrash Rabbah*, Exod. 15, 28)[59]

Let us quote a few complementary examples.

"Now this is what you shall offer on the altar" (Exod. 29:38). The text itself specifies: "new lambs, two a day, always" (ibid.). This rhetorical construction requires explanation: "'Now this is what you shall offer': the laws of ritual slaughtering [appeared obscure to Moses, until the Lord *showed him* the (concrete) procedure] as the verse says: 'Now this (*zot*) is what you shall offer on the altar'" (*Menahoth* 29a).

Or again, concerning the census in the wilderness, carried out by means of a symbolic redemption in money: "This (*zeh*) is what everyone who is entered in the records shall pay: a half-shekel by the sanctuary weight" (Exod. 30:13).

"This is what everyone shall pay": here again, the biblical text puts in a colon, whereas the Jerusalem Talmud interprets

(*Shekalim* 1, 4): "Rabbi Meir taught: the Holy One, blessed-be-He, took a coin [made] of fire from under the throne of His majesty, which he *showed* to Moses as a model: 'This is what everyone shall pay.'"

Inadequation. The problems raised by many of these examples can be reconsidered in the perspective of the inadequation they assume between the use of *zeh* and an abstract term ("the making of the lampstand," "the month"), or perhaps even, if one admits that *zeh* points toward a textual unit, the inadequation between its occurrence and the (notional) content it points to.

In a more general way, as we have said, Midrash *normalizes* in these cases the unexpected occurrence of *zeh* by reinstating its "deep reference" in terms of a concrete and visible object. Thus it once again inverts the relation of determination. In the semantic irregularity of this construction (*zeh* plus abstract noun, hidden or distant reference), it is not the deictic that is questioned, as one might expect, but rather the *object* it designates and on which it depends grammatically: the thematization of the "concrete meaning" of *zeh* is primary and decisive with respect to the reference it qualifies.

This mode of interpretation is clearly visible in the previously cited case of the moon: "The Holy One, blessed-be-He showed him the moon, as it is said: 'This very month (*zeh*) shall mark for you the beginning of the months'" (*Midrash Rabbah,* Exod. 15:28). This version is completed by the *Mekhilta* (6L, 11–12): "This very month: Moses showed the children of Israel the moon when it was new, giving it to them as a sign of the beginning of the month." *Zeh:* the month is a concept, the moon a visible object. This derivation from the abstract to the concrete, from the idea to the act, can be considered characteristic of Jewish tradition.

A second example represents the burial of Jacob in Canaan, during an important procession of his family and Egyptian notables from the land of Goshen to the banks of the Jordan: "When they came to Goren ha-Atad, which is beyond the Jordan, they held there a very great and solemn lamentation; and he observed a mourning period of seven days for his father.

And when the Canaanite inhabitants of the land *saw* the mourning at Goren ha-Atad, they said, 'This (*zeh*) is a solemn mourning on the part of the Egyptians'" (Gen. 50:10–11).

"This is a solemn mourning: Rabbi Yudan, ben Rabbi Shalom, adds the following lesson: this expression teaches us that they *pointed* [at the body] *with their fingers*, saying: 'This man is the cause of great mourning for Egypt'" (*Yerushalmi, Sotah* 1, 10). Mourning is an internal feeling, which cannot be *designated*. What the Canaanites are talking about is Jacob as a person, and the *manifestations* of mourning that are devoted to him.

Or again: "This (*zeh*) is the book of Adam's line. When God created man, He made him in the likeness of God" (Gen. 5:1). "This is the book: Resh Lakish is astonished: did the first man really have a book? But it is in order to teach us that the Holy One, blessed-be-He *showed* him each generation with its exegetes, each generation and its sages" (*Avodah Zarah* 5a). The exegetical translation here is somewhat different, since it rejects an initial concrete reference for another, the criterion being drawn from a *visual* lesson: rather than give it up, Gemara's commentary does not hesitate to resort to prophetic fable.[60]

In a homologous way, in another type of "inadequation," Midrash intervenes when *zeh* appears in association with a noun designating an object situated outside the field of communication, and thus invisible *to the interlocutors*, although in itself it is perceptible and concrete: "When the people saw that Moses was so long in coming down from the mountain, the people gathered against Aaron and said to him, 'Come make us a god who shall go before us, for that man Moses (*zeh*), who brought us from the land of Egypt—*we do not know what has happened to him*'" (Exod. 32:1). The Midrash (*Midrash Rabbah*, Num. 15:21) recounts that when Moses climbed Mount Sinai to receive the Tables of the Covenant, he had promised the children of Israel that he would come back at the end of forty days. "At the end of forty days [since Moses had not returned], Satan said to Israel: Moses is dead. But they paid no attention, until he *showed* them the form of his deathbed. Then they came and said to Aaron: 'for that man Moses . . .'" (*Shabbath* 89a).

RECOGNITION

This thematics of visible presence is broadened by commentary and extended to all modes of cognition and recognition. By its relational nature, this new sememe founds a category intermediary between signalization and thematization. It indicates simultaneously a relationship (of "cognition") to the object, and/or a sign-value ("recognizable") that is supposed to be intrinsic to it.

Obscurity of Referentialization. A first meaning of "recognize" is acknowledgment. It is exploited in the following example of the obscurity of the reference, in which it plays a "signaletic" role (concerning the accusation of theft made against a man the plaintiff had entrusted with his property): "In all charges of misappropriation—pertaining to an ox, an ass, a sheep, a garment, or any other loss, whereof one party alleges, 'this is it' (*zeh*)—the case of both parties shall come before God" (Exod. 22:8). "One party alleges, 'This is it': we learn therefrom that the acknowledgment of the accused [as far as civil law is concerned] is worth the testimony of a thousand other witnesses not directly involved" (*Kidushin* 65b). *Torah Temimah* explains: "the formulation whereby one party alleges, *This is it*, indicates a partial recognition of the crime. The person who was entrusted with the property recognizes 'this' as what he is accused of having lost."[61]

Redundancy. Here now are some typical normalizations of redundancy. The Halakhah[62] bases itself on this general value of recognition to rule on the previously cited case of the wayward son: "This son of ours [*zeh*] is disloyal and defiant" (Deut. 21:20). "One beats him. If he does it again, one gives him a first warning before three witnesses and condemns him to further beating. . . . He is lapidated[63] only in the presence of the *first* three witnesses, according to what is written: 'This son of ours': *the very one whom you saw beaten the first time*" (*Sifré*, Deut. 252 L 9–102, and *Sanhedrin* 71a).

Similarly, a second midrashic interpretation of the verse "Here is the book of Adam's line" (Gen. 5:1) proposes the following reading: "Rabbi Tanhuma teaches in the name of Rabbi Elazar, and Rabbi Menahem in the name of Rav: The first man had learned all the arts. . . . Our Sages add: even calligraphy— in accordance with the expression of the verse: 'here is the book,' which designates the book and ['here is'] its writing" (*Midrash Rabbah*, Gen. 24:7). The commentator on the midrash[64] illuminates the linguistic logic of this explanation: "*Here* is the book: the letters were *perfectly recognizable*, whence one infers that Adam had written them." The presence of *zeh*, which is superfluous for immediate comprehension, thus refers to a surplus of information, which Midrash connects with the writing.

A final example of this series amalgamates the polarities of recognition and visualization:[65] "The daughter of Pharaoh came down to bathe in the Nile. . . . She spied the basket among the reeds. . . . When she opened it she saw that it was a child. . . . She took pity on it and said 'This (*zeh*) must be a Hebrew child'" (Exod. 2:5–6): "'This must be a Hebrew child': how did she *recognize* it? Rabbi Yossef, son of Rabbi Hanina, teaches: She *saw* that he was circumcised" (*Midrash Rabbah*, Exod. 1:24).

Inadequation. This thematic fixation on the object as visible and knowable culminates in man's designation of a hidden God inaccessible to our senses. Nevertheless, we find several examples of the name of the Lord associated with the demonstrative. What then? Must we reconsider the distribution of *zeh* and its meanings in use? Midrash chooses the inverse attitude, subordinating, so to speak, theology to grammar, accounting for the use of the deictic through a relation of proximity to God: "In the garden of Eden, the Holy One, blessed-be-He sits among the Just, and each of them points to him *with his finger*,[66] as it is said (Isa. 25:9): 'This (*zeh*) is our God'" (*Ta'anith* 31a).

This God, revealed to the just, also reveals Himself to the least of the servants during the crossing of the Red Sea: "*zeh Eli*: 'Here is my God, I do Him homage'" (Exod. 15:2). "Here is my God: Rabbi Berakhiah taught us: See the greatness of those who went down to the sea. Moses, how he prayed and begged God, until he was allowed to see His appearance. . . .[67] The angels, the throne-bearers, themselves did not recognize it. . . .

And those who came back up from the sea could each point to Him with their fingers and say: 'Here is my God, I do Him homage'" (*Midrash Rabbah*, Exod. 23:15).

The God of Midrash is a God close to men's expectations, sensitive to experience and memory, who brings about, through His intervention in history, the "recognition" of His kindness. It is in this same, almost familiar mode that another version of Midrash comments on the same verse:

> Here is my God: Rabbi Avira recounts: It is through the virtue of their women that the children of Israel were saved from Egypt. When the women went to draw water, the Holy One, blessed-be-He made little fish come into their pitchers, so that they drew up half water and half fish; they fed their husbands and entered into union with them; and when the time came for the child to be born, they went to give birth in the fields, and the Holy One, blessed-be-He sent them from the heavens someone to wash them and take care of them, just as an animal takes care of its offspring. And when the Lord revealed Himself on the sea, it was the women who recognized Him first, as it is said: "*Zeh Eli*: Here is my God."
>
> (*Sotah* 11b)

To adopt Buber's terms, this God in the modality of revelation is a God to whom one says Thou.

Gematria (the Value 12)

Finally, we might connect these ambivalent techniques of inversion with an unusual hermeneutic procedure based on the numeric value of the letters that make up each word: this is the exercise of *gematria* (or geometry), which infers from these calculations numeric equivalents with signifying effects. Applied to the demonstrative, this exegetical principle bases its explanation on the sole presence of the demonstrative. The latter indicates *numeric coefficient* 12, so to speak, which is attached to one of the elements of the context, or specifically connected, as a *qualifier*, to the designated reference. For example, our Sages draw from the occurrence of *zeh* in the verse "This (*zeh*) shall be a sacred anointing oil" (Exod. 30:31) a clue to the quantity of sacred oil prepared for the inauguration of the sanctuary: "It was twelve cubits, according to the numeric value of the word *zeh*" (*Horayoth* 11b, *Kerithoth* 5b). In the same way, according to the teaching of Gemara,[68] *zeh* adds information concerning the graphic composition of the divorce contract, which has twelve lines.

The same type of reasoning is extended to the composite forms of the demonstrative that include affixes brought into the calculation: "Disperse yourselves among the people, Saul went on, and tell them that every man must bring me his ox or his small animal, slaughter it *here* (or "with this": *bazeh*), and eat it" (1 Sam. 14:34): "Slaughter it here (*bazeh*): B(2) + Z(7) + H(5): Saul showed them a sacrificial knife fourteen fingers long, according to the count of the word *bazeh*" (*Midrash Rabbah*, Lev. 25:8).

By its functioning, *gematria* can thus be classified among the forms of syntactical autonomization examined above. Moreover, we shall see that its calculations lead, on the kabbalistic level, to a general symbolics of numbers (the number 12 representing, for example, in the Judaic configuration, the twelve "dimensions" of the universe), which recalls the process of thematization already studied. However, it clearly differs from these analyses in its formal character, by taking into account a signifying plane discontinuous with respect to the signifieds involved in the discourse. To this extent, it is thus not oriented, according to our definition, toward the *sense* of the demonstrative, in the strict and classic sense of the term.

We glimpse, through these mechanisms, the first signs of a disorder in the exercise or application of the deictic principle of *referential indetermination*. The pertinent traits of sense are so precisely accentuated, and drawn off toward new definitional sememes, that the initial multivalence of the demonstrative as well as its functioning as a "token-reflexivity" seem to be affected. This mutation is the effect of a second orientation of exegesis and of a new grammatical hierarchy, in which we see the progressive impact of ideological presuppositions. Putting the semantic weight of the sentence on the demonstrative, it tends to filter out—already on the level of the language, that is, on the basis of a matrix model—a specific field of the possible references of *zeh*.

This systematic preference accorded to sense can be interpreted—in a first register of analysis—as the establishment and acknowledgment of an autonomous *subjacent code*, a "value added" to the linguistic system to which the text is ultimately subordinated, and defined *prior* to discourse and as if outside it. Here appear the first signs of a *parallel functioning* of the sense of words in the sacred language, drawing on a level of independent *extratextual* signification, corollary to the basic linguistic system.

This new system founds a "second sense" (indicated as S2) parasitical on the first (the classic demonstrative sense, indicated as S1), which develops out of it and systematizes its data according to a process of progressive autonomization. The first of these stages, that of "restriction," is more abstract and allows a functional utilization; the second, that of "proximity" (visualization, recognition), is more concrete and thematic. In both cases, however, in spite of the *discrimination* of references by the sense, which restricts the field of their application, we remain here within the limits of an indeterminate referential play.

In the next chapter, we move beyond the linguistic system toward discourse, seeking, beneath the examination of the actual fixations of *zeh* in the textual fabric of the Bible, a hermeneutic law of references "in situation," corollary to the rules of sense (= referential virtualities) indicated up to this point.

2

The Semantics of References

The preceding chapter gave us a glimpse of a semantics of demonstrative meaning preceding contextualization and having
a more powerful effect. In particular, if the punctual reference
offered by the immediate context is in fact deciphered (Peshat) or symbolically extended (Derash)[1] *on the basis of* the
sense—in conformity with the "natural" play of the language—
we have seen that in the case of a problematic semanticization
priority was given to the demonstrative sememe, whose claims
took precedence over the actual "realizations" of *zeh* in context.

A second orientation of exegesis adopts the inverse procedure, since it reinserts the demonstrative into the whole of the
discourse and bases the recognition of the signification of *zeh*
on its *present* references. This is a complementary procedure
that in effect no longer subjects discourse to language but rather
subjects language to discourse. The exact reference of *zeh* is
determined each time "in situation" and its meaning derived
from this usage.[2]

We shall distinguish two techniques of referential determination by context, one punctual, the other allusive—that is, extended to several cases of utterance.

PUNCTUAL SEMANTICIZATION

The "syntagmatic" semanticization of *zeh*, a natural operation of
clarifying the semantic relations between the demonstrative
and its environment in a given utterance, is normally admitted by talmudic and midrashic commentary. Thus "[the word]
zot refers *specifically* to the Torah, *in accord with the verse*: 'This
is the Torah that Moses set before the Israelites' (Deut. 4:44)"
(*Avodah Zarah* 2b). This is an identification sufficiently strong

to be reconfirmed several times, on the basis of the same example, in rabbinical literature: *Midrash Rabbah*, Deuteronomy 11:4, and *Menahoth* 53b.

Other semantic correspondences are established, such as the one that sees in *zeh* a direct evocation of the Lord, according to the verse "Here (*zeh*) is my Lord, I do him homage (Exod. 15:2) (*Menahoth* 53b and Zohar A 228a or *Vayehi* 118, 379). The same passage in Gemara infers from the verse "For that (*zeh*) man Moses" (Exod. 32:1) a specific determination of *zeh* by the reference "Moses" (*Menahoth* 53b).

According to the form and the force of the articulation of the demonstrative to its context, this relation is based on a genuine grammatical agreement—as in the preceding cases—or instead on an indirect semantic connection. Thus in the example "[The word] *zot* refers strictly to 'circumcision,' as said in the verse 'Such (*zot*) shall be the covenant which you shall keep: you shall circumcise every male among you'" (Gen. 17:10) (*Midrash Rabbah*, Exod. 23:12). The agreement of *zot* with "covenant" is here extended to its cataphoric elaboration:[3] "circumcise every male . . ."

One will have noticed the particularity of these midrashim, which do not limit themselves to making the punctual reference of *zeh* explicit in a given verse but seek to systematize its results. This amounts to a stiffening-up of the referential play that seizes the instantaneous character of an episodic relation to institute it as a feature of sense attached to the demonstrative, in the form of a systematic connotation.

In fact, these *punctual* analyses are not typical of Midrash properly so called. Usually they are conducted by Midrashic commentaries that are kabbalistic in inspiration ("*al pi hakabbalah*") and as such naturally oriented toward a codification of sense effects—which would explain the systematic nature, more or less strongly stressed, of the identification pointed out. This underlying codification makes it possible to rule on *isolated* individual cases without calling on any counterexample. At the same time it legitimates certain liberties taken in the syntactical coordination of the themes.[4] One will note, in the following examples, the *indirect* semanticizations of the demonstrative, which are not easily acceptable on the strictly linguistic level and are sometimes made even more clearly problematic by a very loose contextual fabric: "The rainbow is termed *zot*, as is shown in the verse: 'That (*zot*) shall be the covenant' (Gen. 9:17) [assimilated by the context to the rainbow]" (*Naftulé Vayehi*).[5] The determination of *zeh* as *mizvah*, "commandment," is drawn from an anaphoric reading of Ecclesiastes 12:13: "Fear God and obey His commandments (*mizvothav*), for this (*zeh*) is the whole duty of man" (*Ir Giborim, Bo*).[6]

Other displacements of the grammatical antecedent will thus be admitted, such as those that connect *zeh* with *Torah* in the expression "*This book* of the *Torah* (*Sefer hatorah hazeh*)," where the demonstrative agrees grammatically with the word *book* (*Ir Giborim, Bo*, on Deut. 31:26).

Still more indirectly, "Joseph" is associated with the pronoun *zeh* through the mediation of a contextual thematics, since it is "in the narrative of its history that the expression appears: *nase'u mizeh*, 'They have gone from here' (Gen. 37:17)" (*Zeor Hamor, Vayehi*).[7]

Neither does the uncertain character of these connections prevent the commentator from recognizing "Israel" as a possible referential projection of *zeh*, through two verses noted by the Midrash: "By *zeh*, Israel fell, as it is written: 'For that (*zeh*) man Moses' (Exod. 32:1) [and the context of the passage is that of the sin of the golden calf], and by *zeh*, Israel rose up, as it is written; 'This (*zeh*) is what everyone will pay' [for the construction of the tabernacle] (Exod. 30:13)" (*Midrash Rabbah*, Lev. 8:1; the referential determination is established, on the basis of this midrash, by the *Sefer Erké Hakinuyim*, entry *zeh*).

INTERTEXTUAL SEMANTICIZATION

However, midrashic technique properly so called, which does not claim to have any preceding semantic code and is supposedly based only on the immediate givens of the discourse, is necessarily more circumspect in its processes of identification: the punctual reading cannot suffice to support it. Through a system of evaluation that is peculiar to it, midrashic exegesis

tends rather to construct its commentary on examples in series, on returns of meaning, discerning in them the laws of semanticization, a statistics of contexts. Most of the midrashim
calculating the reference or references of *zeh* are thus based on
the juxtaposition of at least two different occurrences.

We must note first that even the examples of punctual determination already cited usually result from an artificial break-
ing down of complex midrashim into independent elements of
sense, such as the series (Judah, Jerusalem, circumcision, tithes,
sacrifices, tribes, *sabbath*, levies [given to the priests]) cited by
the *Sefer Erké Hakinuyim* (which is kabbalistic in inspiration, and
repeats word for word the references given overall by the Midrash Rabbah [Lev. 21:6]).[8]

Similarly, in this midrash the relation "*zeh*—Israel" passes
through a third verse of reference, which serves as a pivot for
the argument: "It is God who is the judge: He puts down one
(*zeh*) and lifts up another (*zeh*)" (Ps. 75:8). The identification
"*zeh*—Moses" is also supported by testing it on a second verse:
"Moses spoke to the heads of the Israelite tribes, saying: 'This
(*zeh*) is what the Lord has commanded (Num. 30:2) (*Sifré*, Num.
198 L 13)."[9]

In its classical form, the determination of the references of *zeh*
on the basis of the context thus deploys its analysis over much
more extensive utterances. The methodological principle of this
level of interpretation based on the message, and where one
can recognize the *Remez*, or allusion, of traditional exegesis,[10]
is in fact above all *intertextuality*. The allusive reading associates in absentia utterances that it commits to memory, and
makes possible a series of semantic operations based on the
compared (and recurrent) references of the demonstrative.

The commentary proceeds by superimposing contexts, and
we shall see that it ends up by gradually revealing certain
rules of distributivity. Ultimately, its task will be to systematize, over the whole of the corpus, the inventory of the actual references of *zeh* and to derive from them a "semantics of
references."

This technique of carrying over, and the "anaphorization"
that it presupposes, produces another distortion of the deic-

tic force of the demonstrative, which implied, on the contrary, that reference would begin ever anew. A first series of examples will make clear the exegetical consciousness of an interdependence of contexts, a kind of system of combination that would support most of the hermeneutic techniques based on discourse, and in comparison with which the semanticization of the demonstrative constitutes only a particular case.

The technique of allusion consists first of all in the recognition of a contextual translation: *zeh* connotes, as it were, a second context that serves as a semantic complement to the first and makes it possible to complete a reading of it. Here there is no effect of symbolization, or of the superimposition of a figural meaning on the literal meaning, such as a certain definition of Derash (parabolic interpretation), for example, allowed us to anticipate, but rather the elucidation of an immediate context through an antecedent context, almost in the grammatical sense of the term "antecedent." The referentialization is internal to the discourse, since the second utterance refers precisely to the first, in a sort of pronominal textual relation.[11]

For example, it is by allusion that commentary resolves the problem[12] of the emphatic use of *zeh* in the following idiomatic turn of phrase (interrogative pronoun + *zeh*): "Esau said, 'I am at the point of death, so (*Lama-zeh*) of what use to me is my birthright?'" (Gen. 25:32): "Resh Lakish taught: Esau began to blaspheme. The text does not read 'what use to me' but 'so (*zeh*) of what use to me is my birthright,' whence we learn that he has denied [the text] '*zeh Eli*' ('This is my God,' Exod. 15:2) [and its contextual signified]" (*Midrash Rabbah*, Gen. 63:13). *Zeh* represents here a pronominal (anaphoric) turn of phrase, which is related to the whole of the context of signification of the second occurrence of *zeh* and integrates it into the comprehension of the first.

The second example, on Psalms 27:3: "[David praying to God]: 'Let an army encamp against me—the army of the Malekites— / my heart shall not fear,' 'though war—the war of the Malekites—arise against me, / yet I will be confident' [literally, in this (*Bezoth*) I have confidence]": "*Bezoth* [ambiguity or redundancy]: Rabbi Levi taught: in *this*, in the testament that

Moses left us in his Torah, and where he tells the elders (Deut. 33:7): 'And this (zot) concerning Judah'" (Midrash Rabbah, Lev. 21:2). Here again, the object proper of David's "confidence" is an earlier utterance that the term introduces: it is Moses' testament to Judah, a benediction formulated *in the same terms*, that strengthens David's courage in the face of danger.

> This (zot) came to us from the Lord (Ps. 118:23). "*This* (zot) came to us from the Lord, and it is marvelous in our eyes": This verse is related to the text of the Song of Solomon: "What is this (zot) coming up from the wilderness?" [Another possible literal translation is: Who is this woman, coming up from the wilderness?] Formerly, they were enslaved by mortar and bricks, and now here in the wilderness they have become a people, settled in four camps! And Israel replies: We ourselves are astonished by what is happening to us, and the Holy Spirit adds: "*This* came to us from the Lord."
>
> (*Yalkuth Shimoni* 2:876)[13]

The ambiguity of the text, which plays, as we have already seen, on the grammatical ambivalence between the feminine and neuter forms of zot, is undone by the replacement of zot in the new context by its initial contextual environment. Zot is thus identified, through the event of the departure from Egypt, as referring to the (feminine) identity of Israel in the modality of deliverance.

One might thus summarize the technique of the preceding examples by imagining one text as embedded within the other, the former being connoted by the common term zeh or zot, which occurs in both verses. Here the referentialization is internal, intertextual in the literal sense of the term.

MODALITIES OF TRANSLATION

But if the mapping of one text onto another always remains semantic in character, it nonetheless occurs on different levels of integration, according to whether it includes a purely signaletic function (of co-referentiality) or the *thematic* paradigm of the references actually reconstructed on the basis of the contexts selected.

A typical example of polyvalent recurrence (both textual and thematic) may illustrate the extent and nature of this translation. It is cited by *Midrash Rabbah*, concerning the final blessing Moses gives the children of Israel at the moment of his death and before his replacement by Joshua at the border of the Promised Land: "This (*vezoth*) is the blessing with which Moses, the man of God, bade the Israelites farewell before he died" (Deut. 33:1): "This (*zot*) is the blessing: how did Jacob finish his blessing? With the word *zot*, as in the verse (Gen. 49:28): 'And this (*vezoth*) is what their father said to them as he bade them farewell and blessed them.' When Moses wanted to bless Israel, he chose to begin with this same term, according to the text of the verse: This (*vezoth*) is the blessing" (*Midrash Rabbah*, Deut. 11:1).

Another version takes up the same theme: "This is the blessing: the latter is added to the first one, given by Jacob to Israel. The formulation of the verse signifies to us that Moses is opening his peroration at the point where his ancestor closed his, as it is written: This (*vezoth*) is the blessing" (*Sifré*, Deut. 392 L 17; see also *Tanhuma Vayehi* 16).

In an allusive manner, Moses' vision is thus inscribed in the line of Jacob's vision, in a relation of subordination marked by the double occurrence of the word *zot*—a link-relay that makes it possible to connect the Mosaic utterance with the previously cited one in Genesis.

This textual relativization does not, however, exclude a *thematic identification*. The blessing designated by *zot* in Moses' testament is indeed *the very one* that Jacob intended, and concerning which Ramban[14] tells us that the patriarch had promised it would take effect on the day when Israel received the Torah, that is, in the time of the legislator. In the Midrash's rereading, Moses' last words, which are placed under the authority of Jacob, are thus not indifferent in their sources: the lexical continuity is here the sign of an identity of values. Through a similar process, the Midrash demonstrates the unity and the perennial nature of the blessing of Israel, from Abraham to Jacob and Moses. Given by Moses, it becomes the Blessing, always the same, from the Fathers up to the Master, repeated under the name of *zot*. Internal referentialization is thus a source of coherence and unification; it organizes and hierarchizes the textual material into foci of signification.

On the basis of this first analysis, we will be led to consider, for our study of the referentializations of *zeh*, two modes of contextual identification, one formal and almost mathematical, the other properly thematic. These two modes will be seen as two stages of the same process:[15] (a) the factorization of a common reference or a referential context (in Hebrew: *gezerah shavah*),[16] and then (b) the thematic determination of this reference in a paradigmatic series or a distributional class.

At this stage, the particular phenomenon of internal referentialization that marked the actual translation and the intertextual connotation from one utterance to another is broadened to a general effect of co-referentiality. The text's autodesignation, along with the consequences it has for referential elucidation, is here transcended in the direction of a more extensive hermeneutic view. Co-referentiality brings out an actual identity of the references in the pair of utterances in question, without however presupposing a prior carryover from one text to the other.

Functionalization
(or "Signalization": Co-referentiality)

Two parallel utterances, carrying the same morphological "signal," *zeh* or *zot*, appear linked to a single external reference (for example, to a *single* existential situation) in a sort of coordination of contexts. The equivalence is then signaled by the presence of the demonstrative, its meaning-content being deduced from one of the contexts. In the following examples, the comparison occurs in an overall manner, from paragraph to paragraph, the demonstrative serving only as a starter and making it possible to assimilate atypical signifying wholes.

To the extent that no specific investment of the demonstrative as such is produced here—at least on first inspection—we will speak of a *function* of co-referentiality rather than of a thematic determination properly so called. The equivalence, at whatever level it operates, seems to have used a formal identity (the repetition of *zeh*) as only a pretext for inferring a chance referential coincidence. This semantic identification, actual but ephemeral, could not lead to any permanent feature of sense attached by definition to the demonstrative, and which would follow it in each occurrence. A slightly deviant deictic functioning, but one that still preserves an opening up of the reference, remade and unmade through each pair of examples and renewable in spite of its partial neutralization through the exercise of intertextuality: "This very month (*hazeh*) shall mark for you the beginning of the months" (Exod. 12:2): "This very month: Rabbi Assi taught in the name of Rabbi Yohanan: Blessing the month in its time [that is, at the time of the new moon] amounts to welcoming the Presence; one should in fact compare the expression employed here, 'This very month,' with the one that figures in this other context: 'This is my God (*zeh*), I do Him homage'" (Exod. 15:2) (*Sanhedrin* 42a).

An existential equivalence is thus established: it is a matter of the same religious experience, the same kind of spiritual sensibility rendered by the double presence of *zeh*, and made explicit in the archetypical context of the departure from Egypt: "Here is my God." This purely functional, signaletic character of the double occurrence of the term, which is apparently without "intrinsic" justification on the level of the content, has been exploited above all on the level of the Halakhah, through what tradition calls *gezerah shavah*, or linguistic equation.[17]

Jewish hermeneutics based its deductive technique on co-referentiality. This logical-institutional operation rests on a partial identification of the (contextual) references of two extracts containing the same term or the same expression. The word—not necessarily deictic or demonstrative—functions as a signal, as an index of identity. It is at this level, moreover, that tradition acts, retaining the memory of the signal and not that of its semantic investment: there is a referential coincidence, but the content of this coincidence is not precisely defined, and neither are the limits of its application. Picking out two identical terms makes it possible to determine a corollary identity of part of the contexts of signification. This part is freely determined by interpretation. The semantic syllogism thus operates in a global fashion and bears on a whole segment, rather than on the common term and its reference:[18]

> On the third new moon after the Israelites had gone forth from the land of Egypt, on that very day (*bayom hazeh*) they entered the wilderness of Sinai (Exod. 19:1): That very day: the turn of phrase using "very" is also found in a second context (Exod. 12:1): "This very month (*hazeh*) shall mark for you the beginning of the months"; here, as in the other case, it is therefore a matter of the first day of the month; whence one deduces that it is on the day of the new moon that they entered the wilderness of Sinai.
>
> (*Shabbath* 86b)

> On the tenth day of this month each of them shall take a lamb to a family. . . . You shall keep watch over it until the fourteenth day of this month; and all the aggregate community of the Israelites shall slaughter it at twilight. . . . They shall eat the flesh that same night (*hazeh*) (Exod. 12:3–8). They shall eat the flesh that same night (. . .): Rabbi Elazar ben Azaria teaches: the same expression, "that same night" (*balaylah hazeh*) is found later on (Exod. 12:12): "For that night I will go through the land of Egypt and strike down every first-born in the land of Egypt": just as it is a question, in the second passage, of the first part of the night (up until midnight), in this passage, flesh shall be eaten . . . up until midnight.[19]
>
> (*Berakhoth* 9a)

> The Lord spoke to Moses in this way: Speak to Aaron and his sons, and to all the Israelite people and say to them: *This is what* [literally, 'here is the thing,' *zeh hadavar*] the Lord commanded: If any man of the house of Israel slaughters an ox or sheep or goat, or does so outside the camp, and does not bring it to the entrance of the Tent of Meeting to present it as an offering to the Lord, before the Lord's Tabernacle, bloodguilt shall be imputed to that man: he has shed blood.
>
> (Lev. 17:1–4)

To follow the somewhat more complex reasoning of this last example, we will cite here the passage with which it is placed in a relation of partial equivalence. It appears immediately that these two extracts are absolutely heterogeneous from the point of view of their referential context, which makes more manifest the mathematical character of the operation, at least on first inspection: "Moses spoke to the heads of the Israelite tribes, saying: This is what the Lord has commanded: If a man makes a vow to the Lord or takes an oath imposing an obligation on himself, he shall not break his pledge; he must carry out all that has crossed his lips" (Num. 30:2–3). And here is the Gemara's commentary: "*Zeh hadavar* ('this is what'): we find used here '*zeh Hadavar*,' an expression that also occurs in the context of the sacrifices made outside the Tabernacle [cf. the first text]: just as concerning outside sacrifices Moses addresses Aaron, his sons, and *all the Israelite people*, in the same way, concerning vows of abstinence, it is a question of Aaron, his sons, and all the Israelite people. What lesson should the decision makers draw from this? It is that in order to release a man from his vows [second text], a tribunal composed of *any* three members of the Israelite people suffices ['all the Israelite people,' in the first text]. But nevertheless it is written [concerning vows of abstinence] that Moses addressed [specifically] 'the heads of the Israelite tribes' [and not 'all the Israelite people']? That is in order to establish a spiritual authority ['a head of a tribe'] as *one* possible judge" (*Nedarim* 78a).

The clarification added by the *gezerah shavah* bears this time on the person concerned by the command in question. It makes it possible to specify, from a given perspective, the limits of the applicability of the conduct to be followed. However, the equality thus established does not eliminate the immediate contextual divergence of the two passages, which must in turn be accounted for. It will be possible to maintain the conclusion that they are partially equivalent to the extent that the preceding diversity remains justified; that is, to the extent to which the first, nonallusive, reading is validated.[20]

The *gezerah shavah*, and more generally the examples of coreferentiality cited, have in common their bearing on contexts that are general and even *indirectly* linked with the term (*zeh, zot*) brought into play as a catalyst. It therefore seems that only a system of inter(intra-)textual equation is developed, but without the pertinence of the common word as such being implied, at least *apparently*.[21]

We shall summarize by saying that *gezerah shavah* rediscovers, as it did earlier,[22] a functionalization (and an inversion) of the relationship of determination, this determination no longer being punctual but rather relational, no longer linked to a *sense* but to an external *reference*.

Nevertheless, at least, in these two cases, the "empty" word is a source of meaning, through its own linguistic givens, or by relation to other moments of utterance in which it occurs, and whose mark it bears. It is also interesting to note that the semantic freight that emerges a posteriori from the equation is perceived here in the moment at which it is retransmitted and not in the one where it is determined.

Commentary thus presents the actualized substitution. Referential determination, the first stage of the translation, is achieved implicitly to reveal itself only "in relation" through the parallel with a second context. Thus we can verify that generally, in the inventory of Midrash properly so called,[23] there is no punctual determination through the reference in the discourse corollary to the punctual semanticization through the sense. To this extent, the demonstrative remains deictic, "grammatical"; it retains a relative referential mobility. *Zot* signifies what it signifies only in *another* text and not "in itself." The meaning's regression is more important, at this level, than the meaning itself.[24]

On the other hand, this particular capacity of referential connection through a common sign is once again experienced as a determination of the context *by* this sign: since of the two stages of intertextual referentialization (the determination of a meaning, then the transmission of the meaning),[25] it is the latter that is emphasized and privileged. This is a reversal that must be interpreted, as in the first chapter, and in spite of the difference in approach, in terms of semantic presupposition. It is as if the comprehension of the text were subject to other parameters than those of pure discursivity, and recognized, for example, an irregular conditioning of the signification through the presence/absence of key terms such as the demonstrative.[26]

The second sign of a "parallel" regulation of commentary

(turning on the references) has to do with the selective character of the contexts noted. The very fact of a *conventional* limitation, which is imposed by tradition on the exercise of *gezerah shavah*, suggests that a pure play of interpretation would not suffice to ground the practice. Behind the appearances, one must acknowledge that this operation of co-referentialization, codified by exegetical memory, is not arbitrary in its contents, nor is it mechanically linked to any identity of the signifiers whatever.

The conjuncture of these remarks on the channeling of semantic phenomena leads here again to the assumption of the existence of an underlying *referential encoding*[27] centered around the demonstrative, that is, limited to a specific term and to the regulated distribution of its references. This thesis is confirmed in the second stage of analysis, which will bring out a regularity of the themes determined by the demonstrative and will make it possible to extend this referential transitivity to a series of permutable contexts between them, and collected into a coherent paradigm.

Thematic Determination

The first sign of the importance attributed to the content in itself is discernible beneath the rabbis' effort to semantically motivate (that is, semantically motivate *as well*) the formal equation and the projections that it authorizes. This justification of the *specific* references tends to rediscover a rule of signification that transcends, or grounds "in thematic reason," the purely transitive technique: if the comparison is possible, it is because an intention of the sense secretly determines it.

These efforts to reestablish a de facto homology between textual, formal laws and underlying semantic combinations obviously proceeds from a peculiar "faith" in the coherence of the different levels of biblical expression, through which the arbitrariness of the mechanism of referential equation would be reduced. Perhaps it is only with respect to certain contexts that *zeh* is authorized to play this role of catalyst in which its

own semantic valence seems to be reabsorbed. At least, perhaps it is only in certain contexts that this mechanism is made
manifest.[28]

To return to our first example, "Blessing the month in its time
[= at the time of the new moon] amounts to welcoming the
Presence" (*Sanhedrin* 42a),[29] as we have said, the identity of religious experiences—whether direct, as in the revelation concerning the Red Sea, or indirect, through the completion of the
ritual of the blessing of the moon—is *conventionally* conveyed
by the word. The commentator of the *Torah Temimah*,[30] Rabbi
Barukh Halevi Epstein, explains the moral sense of this comparison in a different way: "this equivalence rests on the fact
that the renewal of the moon manifests the Lord's mastery
over the world, and the renewal that He brings to it; the man
who blesses the month thus bears public witness to the divine
Sovereign, and celebrates His glory. The same elements appear in the teaching of the verse 'This is my God, I do him
homage'; they saw His Glory *manifested* on the sea." The textual identification thus has an ethical foundation, even if it is
the formal identity that sets the mechanism in movement.

In general, posttalmudic commentators raised the question
of the coherence and pertinence of these comparisons on the
level of content, with a concern, typical of the tradition, to bring
together the logical reasoning with the values that it puts in
play.[31]

One can thus envisage going beyond the demonstration of a
pure (formal) transitivity of the reference to examine its *thematic recurrence*. It is only at this level that it will be really a
question of referential *identity*. If the same word, picked out in
two contexts, refers to the same entity—the implicit reference
being deduced from the explicit reference—this reference is
not arbitrary but manifests an element of sense *attached* to the
common term. Thus is produced *stricto sensu* a phenomenon
of referential *determination* radically contrary to deictic norms,
since the punctual reference of the demonstrative *is integrated*
into its sense to *accompany it in new contexts*. So much so that
one finds oneself endowed with a sort of paradigmatic class
of the possible references—taken two by two—of the word

zeh. This class is organized in a *referential field* that, as we shall see, possesses its own logic and a specific thematic unity.

THE REFERENTIAL
FIELD OF THE DEMONSTRATIVE

Our illustration will follow Midrash's preferences, organizing around *zot* a global, privileged field.

The Semantic Constellation of Zeh

The semantic constellation of *zeh* must in fact be first *reconstituted* on the basis of the midrashim that put its references into play: "Moses said: This (*zeh*) is what the Lord has commanded that you do, that the Presence of the Lord may appear to you" (Lev. 9:6). The midrash recognizes in "this" (*zeh hadavar*) an allusion to a second verse, in which the same expression is made explicit in "circumcision": "What does the expression *zeh hadavar* ('this is what') signify? Moses repeated to them the commandment of circumcision, as it is said in the same terms: *vezeh hadavar*. This is why Joshua had to practice this circumcision (Josh. 5:4)" (*Midrash Rabbah*, Num. 12:8).[32] To sharpen this identification, one could also say that the commentary acknowledges a specific thematization of *zeh* as "circumcision" and that it bases the assertion on a proof-verse.[33]

Neither is there any precise guarantee of a *constituted* thematic circuit in the following example, which is apparently purely functional: "When Moses sent them to scout the land of Canaan, he said to them, 'go that way, toward the hill'" (Num. 13:17): "Go that (*zeh*) way: Moses gave them his *rod* to protect them. The word *zeh*, used here ('that [*zeh*] way') in fact reappears concerning Moses' rod: 'You shall have this (*zeh*) same rod in your hand' (Exod. 4:17)" (R. Bahyé,[34] Exod. 19:24).

Nevertheless, the desire to crystallize the "rod" as a particular semanticization of *zeh* is marked here, even more strongly than the play of equivalence brought into operation, without its being possible to give this proposition, at this stage of the study, more than an intuitive grounding. To which is added, however, the signature of Rabbi Bahyé, an exegete of a mystical bent and inclined for this reason[35] to treat the contents of signification on the same level as the operations that reveal them. This thematization of *zeh*, governed by very precise rules, will be presented as a constituted whole—constituted by exegesis itself—only in subsequent chapters. Here it remains conjectural, a matter of statistics.

The Semantic Constellation of Zot

So far as *zot* is concerned, the verification of a possible thematic coherence is facilitated by the fact that the class of its references appears *already* elaborated by the Midrash and is concentrated around two or three archetypical contexts. We recall the equation [*zot* = circumcision] established by *Midrash Rabbah* (see above, p. 48 concerning the comparison of two verses. To this particular identification may be added other isolated cases of semantic equivalences presented as stable: "This (*ve-zoth*) is the blessing with which Moses, the man of God, bade the Israelites farewell before he died" (Deut. 33:1): "This is the blessing: Rabbi Shemuel, son of Nahman, taught: At the moment when Moses came to bless Israel, the Torah and the Lord came to bless Israel with him. 'This (*zot*) is the blessing: *the reference is to the Torah*, just as it is written (Deut. 4:44): 'This (*ve-zoth*) is the Torah that Moses set before the Israelites'" (*Midrash Rabbah*, Deut. 11:4).

What becomes immediately significant is that the same results are set forth, through new equivalences, by other commentators: Rabbi Bahyé does in fact identify *zot* with *Torah*, but on the basis of two entirely different verses: "This is what their father said to them, as he blessed them" (Gen. 49:28): "*Zot* . . . represents the Torah, as it is written: 'This is the procedure (*zot hatorah*) when a person dies in a tent' (Num. 19:14)"[36] (R. Bahyé, Gen. 49:28). To this correspondence, Rabbi Bahyé, basing himself on the Midrash, adds others, such as the already-cited equivalence "*Zot*—Israelite people," that of *zot* and "circumcision," and *zot* and the *terumah* (offering) (R. Bahyé, Gen.

49:28). Here the recurrence becomes clear. Thus one glimpses a structuration of the references in which each particular midrash would find its place.

This hypothesis is confirmed by returning to Bahyé's midrashic source (not cited), which produces a comprehensive thematic unity much broader than the fragmentary determinations selected by the commentator. The verse that serves as a pivot for this reconstruction is striking by its referential indetermination. It is nevertheless an essential verse for the recognition of a thematic category based on *zot*, and often cited: "This is how [literally, 'with this' or 'with this one' or 'like this': *bezoth*] Aaron shall enter the Shrine: with a bull of the herd for a sin offering and a ram for a burnt offering" (Lev. 16:3).

One can read in this verse a cataphoric redundancy, "this" being developed later in the text ("with a bull of the herd . . . "), or as a referential indetermination (once the supererogatory interpretation has been eliminated, for ideological reasons). The commentary is placed before an "empty" term to be invested: it will seek to identify the exact nature of *zot*, more or less considered at this stage as a common noun of precise reference but not yet deciphered: "With *zot*, Aaron shall enter the Shrine."

This identification of the reference is achieved classically by means of translation, the midrash seeking out the contexts of equivalence in which can be recognized the exact designation of *zot*. These contexts are established in a binary manner but end up being organized into a thematic class, a paradigm of possible referential determinations of *zot* in discourse, probably situated, as we shall verify later on, in a general relation of reciprocal *connotation*.[37]

This (*bezoth*) is how Aaron shall enter the Shrine: Rabbi Yudan explains this text by applying it to the entry of the head priest, laden with merits, into the Holy of Holies. And what are these merits [by means of which he shall enter]? The merit of the *Torah*, as it is written: "This [*zot*] is the Torah that Moses set before the Israelites" (Deut. 4:44); the merit of *circumcision*: "Such (*zot*) shall be the covenant which you shall keep: you shall circumcise every male among you" (Gen. 17:10); the merit of the *Sabbath*: "Blessed is the man who does this (*zot*) . . . blessed the man who respects the Sabbath and does not profane it" (Isa.

56:2); the merit of *Jerusalem*, as it is written: "This (*zot*) is Jerusalem" (Ezek. 5:5);[38] the merit of the *tribes*: "This (*vezoth*) is what their father said to them as he blessed them" (Gen. 49:28); the merit of *Judah*: "This (*vezoth*) he said of Judah" (Deut. 33:7); the merit of *Israel*: "This stature (*zot*) that distinguishes you is like that of a palm tree" (Song of Sol. 7:8); the merit of the *Terumah* [an offering for the Shrine]: "This (*vezoth*) is what you shall receive from them" (Exod. 25:3); the merit of the *tithes*: "Bring the full tithes into the storehouse . . . and thereby put Me to the test" (Mal. 3:10); the merit of the *offerings*, as it is written: "This (*bezoth*) is how Aaron shall enter the Shrine" (Lev. 16:3).

(*Midrash Rabbah*, Lev. 21:6)[39]

The series of these semantic possibilities must be considered paradigmatic, that is, as representing a class of terms linked by a sign of alternative (either/or). Nevertheless, the hypothesis of an *inclusive* rather than exclusive alternative must be admitted, the proposal of a general identifying theme, *zot*, *differentiated* into the following elements of meaning or modalities:

- the Torah
- circumcision   ⎫ "signs of covenant" in
- the Sabbath   ⎭ biblical terminology
- Jerusalem
- the twelve tribes
- the assembly of the Israelites
- Judah (royalty)
- commandments linked with the priesthood: the *terumah*, tithes, offerings

We will test the coherence of this referential field deduced from the actual contextualizations of *zot* by comparing this midrash with other, more elliptical versions, which set forth partial or complementary formulations of this first group. Here then, in addition to the binary equivalences mentioned earlier, is a second generic example, which is all the more interesting in that it is attached—setting forth the same thematic categories—to a context with *zeh* and not *zot*:

Here is how [*zeh hadavar*: literally, here is the thing, here is the way] you shall do them in consecrating them to serve Me as priests (Exod. 29:1). Here is how: by what merit did Aaron enter the Shrine? Rabbi Hanina ben Rabbi Yishma'el taught: by the merit of *circumcision,* as it is written (Lev. 16:3): "This is how (*bezoth*) Aaron shall enter the Shrine": this (*zot*) refers to circumcision, as it is said in the verse (Gen. 17:10): "This (*zot*) is the covenant you shall keep" . . . Rabbi Yizhak teaches: by the merit of the *tribes,* as it is said (Exod. 29:1): "Here is how (*zeh hadavar*) you shall do them"; *zeh,* by its numerical value 12, refers to the *twelve* stones that Aaron wore on his pectoral, and which were engraved with the names of the ten tribes . . . so that on the day of the Great Redemption, when Aaron enters the Shrine, the Holy of Holies may see them, and recall the merit of the tribes.

(*Midrash Rabbah,* Exod. 38:8)

What leads us to lean toward the hypothesis of a systematic recurrence of the themes when comparing the two versions is that the *same* elements of signification are isolated, though in distinct contexts and on the basis of new deductions, in order to rediscover axes that are identical if incomplete: here, for example, *circumcision* and the *tribes* alone.

Let us note in these examples the hypothesis of a "tree" of references taken on by the demonstrative. The interdependence of the contextual elements and the organicity they reveal allow us to infer, on the basis of these particular actualizations, beyond the series that brings them into association, the indication of a generic theme of denomination *zeh* or *zot.*[40]

One may ask, before admitting this work of structuration, what its foundations and scope might be. Is this "metatheme" inscribed *in the text,* as the inductive procedure suggests? Is it the focal point of a curve unifying *all* the "referential points" of the occurrences of *zeh?* Having started out following biblical discourse and its actual semanticizations of the demonstrative, we have to acknowledge, first of all, a "structuralist" reading of Midrash, which would seek to discover the law underlying the example and an a posteriori thematic organization of the distribution of *zeh.*

However, the semantic convergence and the intersections among references argue rather for an a priori codification of the theme of the reading, which is discerned in the text through the presuppositions of the commentary.[41] The latter would then *select* the semantic determinations of *zeh* according to a pre-established model of meaning, a paradigm of its possible references, and by virtue of which it is a single signified whole, radiating out around *zeh* (*zot*, in our example), which traverses all the contexts and gives its particular color to each case of utterance. We therefore have a single semantic category, no longer constructed on the basis of its references, but *constructing* its referential projections and determining the contexts on which it bears.[42]

In any case, it is clear that exegesis has its grids, whether reconstructed or prior. We shall posit that this paradigmatic class of references (or "referential field" of *zeh*), which commentary picks up and puts in place, ultimately refers in its turn to a system of references connoted by a second level (indicated as R2), a "deep structure" designated and represented by the whole of the contextual references determined by the demonstrative and emphasized by Midrash.

The analysis of these first two layers of exegesis, one focused on the sense, the other on the references of the demonstrative,[43] shows a linguistic functioning that is more or less normal, or at least theoretically presented as such. The perception of a resistance or recurrence of the commentary is subterranean and does not invalidate in any way the immediate comprehension, the punctual explication in the syntagmatic coherence. In no case (except for the already cited one of *gezerah shavah*)[44] can it claim—at this level—"official" recognition, or restrain or mutilate an autonomous textual labor. The very fact that, by virtue of a very clearly stated principle, the direct meaning of a text possesses an irreducible value[45] and can never be invalidated guarantees the plasticity of a "pure" (exegetical) textual functioning, free from all conventional constraints.

In the next chapter we shall discuss the anagogic level of interpretation, which breaks with these linguistic analyses in that it presents itself first of all in the form of an independent hermeneutic whole, completely divorced from the preceding. However, to the extent that Jewish mysticism has already conceived and prepared a structured space of landmarks, a reservoir from which we can draw on further depths of exegesis, perhaps it will not spoil the "suspense" too much if at this point we hint at a possible intersection[46] of some kind between this already elaborated conventional code, on one hand, and the underlying regulating systems (S_2 and R_2) respectively tracked at lower levels of meaning, on the other.

3

The Coded Level (Sod)

Jewish hermeneutics also acknowledges an "absolute" register of signification, radically cut off from the context of the utterance or act of utterance, and corresponding to the anagogic level of interpretation (Sod). Its characteristic is to propose for each word in the Bible—which thus becomes a lexicon of the universal—a single *proper* reference, independent and determined, chosen from the order of the necessary values that founded the world.

Through its hypothesis of truth, this original and coded a priori reading of the text seems to snare the infinity of meaning in its net. It restores its openness, however, through the inextricable complexity of its thematic networks and functionings—whose principal articulations this chapter marks out.

We have seen that the rabbis of the Midrash and the Talmud did not hesitate, as early as the first stages of exegesis, to use the demonstrative *zeh* or *zot* with an indefinite value—defined formally by its grammatical nature itself ("this one," "that one"), undefined semantically by the absence of any referential precision. As if the reference of a demonstrative were an established fact of the linguistic system itself, a cultural convention that was recognized and locatable in an iterative manner in each of its occurrences; as if a presupposition of referential uniqueness appeared, marked by the use of the demonstrative pronoun, and which only a cultural consensus would make it possible to establish: "Our brothers, you who are weary and weighed down by your mourning, put your heart to searching this one (*zot*), this one remains forever" (*Ketuboth* 8b).

Let us also recall the preliminary formulation of the example drawn from the treatise *Menahoth* 53b:[1] "Let this one (*zeh*) come, and let him receive this one (*zot*) from this One (*zeh*) for this people." The redefinition of these terms, along with the quotation, is not necessary, but ultimately rather redundant, in a decoding that nevertheless remains ambiguous, to the extent to which it does not acknowledge itself as systematic: "Let 'this one' come: a reference to Moses, concerning whom it is said: 'For that man (*zeh*) Moses,' and let him receive 'this one' refers to the Torah, concerning which it is said 'This is (*zot*) the Torah that Moses set [before the Israelites]'; from 'this one' refers to the Holy One, blessed-be-He, concerning whom it is said 'This is (*zeh*) my God, I do him homage'" (*Menahoth* 53b). This is still a polyvalent interpretation, whose multiplicity will be explained as coherence in the course of this chapter.

It is at the anagogic level proper that a specific hermeneutic attitude is set in place: it admits an institutional security in designation and takes as a principle the existence of a "secret meaning" hidden beneath the everyday word, a precise order of correspondences (whose semantic details will be less immediately pertinent here than the mechanism they reveal): "There is in the word *zot* a *secret* which we will reveal later . . . and which must be understood" (Ramban, on Gen. 2:23). "*And according to the way of truth, vezot* ['and here is'] refers to the blessing. . . . I shall explain . . . and the sage will understand . . . for it is to this hidden meaning that our Sages in the midrash of Genesis referred" (Nachmanides, on Deut. 33:1: *Vezoth Haberakhah*). Or again on the verse: "This (*vezot*) is what their father said to them" (Gen. 43:28): "According to the way of the *Kabbalah, zot* [will be interpreted] as designating the Israelite people" (R. Bahyé, commentary on this verse in the Torah).

Henceforth determining each time a definite reference, whose multiplicity of facets we shall see come together in a single unique principle, the demonstrative seems to change its grammatical category, and slip from "indefinite" pronoun into a proper noun. This functional shift is linked to a new quality of the reading, which relates the words to an "origin" of meaning, to the Value[2] that they represent or convey in language. This Value, on the basis of which, as we shall see, secondary significations can be derived, is a first principle of reference; it stamps its mark on the sign and remains as a trace in all the senses that will be taken on by this term.

This redistribution of the primary, original meaning of the universe, in the words of the language, does not exclude any grammatical category: it endows[3] even "empty words" with a primary, necessary, not contingent, reference that is precise and individualized, one of the cornerstones of the spiritual edifice of the world, or, according to the language of Jewish mysticism, one of the essential mediations of the universe, or *Sephirah*.[4]

Ultimately, *zeh* and *zot* thus manifest particularized appellations, the specific modalities of the Creator's expression, the Word through which the absolute is revealed in a given, limited sphere of spiritual experience.[5] We may cite in support of this functional and semantic mutation one of the first post-talmudic kabbalistic texts that identifies the demonstrative as the *proper name* of a *Sephirah*: "And this divine attribute [the tenth and last of the Spheres of truth] is signified in the Torah *by a specific term* . . . and this Sphere *receives the name of zot*."[6]

This last referentialization calls for several comments: first, it seems to break with the hermeneutic continuity of the preceding levels and to propose a new system of correspondences that is freed from all prior thematic conditioning.[7] Above all, it challenges the pertinence of a signified, that is to say a content of signification corollary to the specific reference assumed by each designation. Anagogic reading defines a kind of comprehension that seems to be radically distinct, primary, and discontinuous within the exegetical fabric.

However, the approach to each *Sephirah* through the words that designate it may—as can be seen from the first examples of univocal identification cited—be indirect or refracted. To explain these plural interpretations of *zeh* or *zot*, even in a conventional register, it must be understood that this *proper reference* called for by anagogic reading, and whose precise and absolute character we have stressed, nonetheless does not close the cycle of signification. For according to the division of the mystical this Value referred to by the demonstrative is not a circumscribed or static truth. It is itself double, and presents itself as well through a complex of representations that manifest it, in a paradigm of symbolizations that symbolize each other and refer to a homologous series of linguistic determinations. It therefore presents itself on the contrary and in its turn as an *empty structure*, that is, as a semantic possibility to be actualized. In the mystical system of the relations of signification, each Sphere (and surely this "geometrical" appellation[8] refers to a form rather than a content, to a structure as content) would thus play more or less the role played by the demonstrative in discourse.[9]

In the arrangement of each particular *Sephirah*,[10] we will therefore not be surprised to discover a restricted choice of fundamental traits of sense, a key theme out of which a whole constellation of derived determinations radiates. The tapped motifs are presented as possible illustrations, particular actualizations of this abstract, productive principle.

By metaphor, the terms "sense" and "reference" will be retained to designate these processes of derivation through which a semantic structure that was initially undifferentiated[11] is determined. The exact nature of these references, which is difficult to grasp, is located somewhere at the intersection of a symbolization and a concretization.[12] Again, to guarantee the coherence of the discussion until the dichotomy is resolved in the conclusion, we will treat these references as *signs* that can be envisaged in their double characterization as signifiers and signifieds.

Indeed, the level of Sod "acts" on the terms as well as on the associated concepts. The semantic grids that it proposes are all based on a lexicality of a particular type (since it is totally conventional), but which recognizes that the *word* has sufficient importance to guarantee its articulation with discourse and its reinsertion into the biblical text itself.[13]

We shall also have to inquire into the generating principle of these derivations. By their systematic nature, they cannot be reduced to an "open" referentialization of a linguistic type; nevertheless, they presuppose different and concurrent systems of combination. The schemas presented later on are based on a fundamental thematic-logical actualization, but we will admit other possible paths of derivation to be analyzed at the end of this chapter. Sod is thus itself the space of an ambivalence, divided between the one and the many, the radical and the indeterminate (the real and the conceptual).

As absolute perception, the anagogic reading actually rereads in the Text a transcription of these essential truths; each verse thus puts into play an epic narrative of the universe that must be deciphered, first of all, at its authentic level of signification. This is the immediate designation, for each term of the Bible, of a "proper reference." But at the same time, this ultimate reference designated by the demonstrative is itself atomized by the explosion of a hidden nucleus into partial representations, and can be grasped at the diverse intersections of its designation.

THE THEMATIC TREE
OF THE DEMONSTRATIVE

As they are grasped by the kabbalists, the feminine (*zot*) and masculine (*zeh*) forms of the demonstrative refer to the last two of the ten universal *Sephiroth*, which are assimilated to the ten attributes of God. The tenth *Sephirah*, corresponding to *zot*, is that of *Malkhuth* (Kingdom); the ninth, corresponding to *zeh*, is that of *Yesod* (Foundation). *Zeh* is also sometimes identified with the sphere *Tifereth* (Beauty), the matrix of *Yesod*.[14] (See p. 73.)

This identification is commented on at length by the author of the *Sha'aré Orah*, who spells out its implications.[15] It is sometimes just mentioned, in one or another of the "lexicons" prepared by the kabbalists over the centuries, probably in a pedagogical effort to systematize the informative material drawn out by the tradition. Under the entry "*zeh*" in the *Pardes Rimonim*, for example, concerning the "Value of the denominations," we find these same statements of appurtenance: "One will not be surprised at the connection of *zot* with the sphere of *Malkhuth*, and that of *zeh* with the spheres of *Yesod* and *Tifereth*, as I have explained. For all three are called *Berith*, the covenant."[16]

Among the more recent nomenclatures, that of the Rabbi Yehiel Halperin,[17] or that of *Kehilath Ya'akov*,[18] repeat the same correspondences: "*Zeh* is called *Yesod* . . . but its principle is

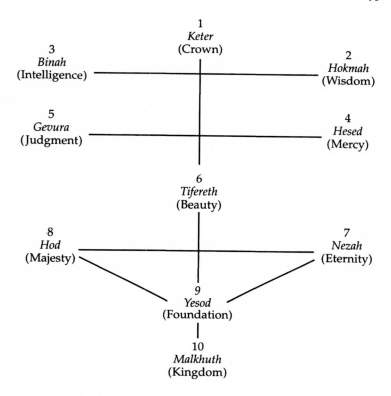

rooted in *Tifereth*."[19] "*Zot*: it is the *Sephirah* of *Malkhuth*." "*Zeh*: *Tifereth* and *Yesod*."[20] But one also finds these same terms, dispersed in the Zohar for example, prior to their systematization into constituted lists: "*Zeh*: *Yesod* and *zot*: *Malkuth*."[21] These are convergent traditions that all connect the demonstrative with the two inferior *Sephiroth*.[22]

We will first present, in the wake of each sphere, the thematic class referred to by the demonstrative, in a sort of tree of signification with growing branches. Let us recall that the totality of the representations covered by each *Sephirah* (and which are named through the demonstrative) can be generated out of a fundamental theme, in an organized network of concepts, on a logical or conventional basis and outside of any context.

Here then is a summary (and selective) overview of the thematic complexes subtended by the two spheres of *Yesod* (*-Tifereth*) and *Malkhuth,* which correspond respectively to the denominations of *zeh* and *zot* in the Jewish mystical tradition's taxonomy. Their presentation as a schema, at the end of each analysis, will make comparative evaluations possible.

Since the world of the spheres is hierarchized—or more precisely, oriented on the basis of an originary principle that remains hidden, ineffable, down to the naked spaces of Creation, in the diffusion of the celestial radiation toward the inferior regions—these last two spheres will be recognized as the ones closest to the earth, the only ones accessible, *through revelation,* to human knowledge. They correspond to the perception that man can have of God's actions in the world; they are the expansion of Value into the sensible, the manifested limit of the divine, where the exercise of *representation* can still attach itself. It is by this degree of interference in things and in history that God makes himself known in the double appellation of *zeh* and *zot*. Under the name of *zot*, he is Providence; under the name of *zeh*, he brings Salvation.[23]

Thus we can summarize the preceding perspectives in the generic concept of *Revelation. Zeh* and *zot* designate respectively, with specific qualifications, the modalities in which a God recognized in existential experience reveals himself, an absolute inscribed as a trace in the concrete. This fundamental trait is particularized into elements of meaning in the separate analysis of the semantic paradigms *zeh* and *zot*.

THE THEMATICS OF *Zeh*

The Kabbalah adopts the image of *unveiling* as the symbolic key to the *Sephirah* of *Tifereth,* to which *zeh* refers:

> But in the future, when the Presence returns to its Place, the Lord [lit., the Name] will put off all His coverings and make Himself visible to the eyes of the Israelites, and that is the secret sense of the verse (Isa. 30:20): "Your Teacher will not hide Himself any more, but your eyes shall see him" and of the expression (Isa. 52:8): "They see with their own eyes the return of the Lord to Zion." That is why one finds written (Isa. 25:9): "It

will be said on that day, Lo, this is our God; we have waited for him, that he might save us. This is the Lord; we have waited for him; let us be glad and rejoice in his salvation." What time is referred to here? The time when God takes off his opaque coverings and no longer hides himself from your eyes.

(Sha'aré Orah, p. 97)[24]

It is the impurity flowing from transgression that is an obstacle to knowledge. Beyond these coverings preventing visual transparency, the act of unveiling will make it possible to accede to the essential point. Behind the walls and opacities Being is concealed, which finally becomes visible—through effort for the Good, through the creature's striving for Good. This principle of unveiling is translated on the concrete level by all the modalities of the sign: inscription, appearance, irruption of the transcendent in the order of the world. A transcendence perceived, according to the version, as *centrality* or *totality*: "The Name of the Lord is situated at the *center* . . . and *all* the qualifiers are connected with it, all around it" (*Sha'aré Orah*, p. 129).

This double character is unified in the graphic representation of it given us. The two *Sephirot* of *Tifereth* and *Yesod* are established on the median dividing the outline of the constellation of the spheres.[25] On the right side of this axis are the attributes of Mercy; on the left, those of Judgment. The synthesis (the totality) is actualized along the median axis (centrality): "Open your eyes and consider why the *vav* of the Tetragrammaton (that is, the "median"), which represents the Name, is called "Beauty" (*Tifereth*): it is because this Name of the Lord is Beauty, in that it recapitulates the names and reigns" (*Sha'aré Orah*, p. 123). This principle of totality has a secret number, the number 12, in which the Kabbalah sees recapitulated the twelve dimensions of the universe.[26]

The class of the reciprocal connotations of the *Tifereth-Yesod* complex, to which the demonstrative refers, is formed by the projections of this category onto one or another level of representation (actualization). We shall give only a few examples of these thematic derivations.[27]

In its metaphysical dimension, the *Sephirah* of *Yesod* thus refers above all,[28] through the multiplicity of spiritual mediations, to the *God* of the *unveiling*, the God of deliverance and revelation, the saving and life-giving God, in dialogue with man, and master of man's destiny.

Through the whole of Creation, this sphere is a "sign": "And sometimes this Sphere of *Yesod* is called *ot*, 'the sign,' because it is from it that come the signs and the miracles brought about in the secrecy of 'El-'Haï' [the Name corresponding to the ninth *Sephirah*]" (*Sha'aré Orah*, p. 48). This sign has its symmetrical counterpart in the Law of Israel, through the commandments carried out, which testify to the covenant.[29] Inscribed on the very flesh, this sign becomes the uncovering by circumcision.[30] In the order of History, this sphere is concentrated around the *witness*-event of the *departure from Egypt*, and the revelation in the Sinai. In the order of space, it refers to the place *manifested, Jerusalem*.

Tifereth is more particularly marked by the figure of Moses, who was the only prophet of Israel who encountered God "face to face," "like a man speaking with his friend."[31] *Yesod*, on the other hand, receives the seal of Jacob, a *median* figure between Abraham and Isaac who is gradually torn away from the toils of impurity.[32] Projected onto the ethical plane, this attribute becomes the virtue of truth (*Emeth*), the dividing line between all the directions of moral experience.

The principle of centrality is translated formally by the (median) line,[33] which figures the letter *vav*, the vertical line that also represents the third letter of the Tetragrammaton and that includes, by its place in the alphabet and by its numerical value, the number 6 (or 12) in its own series.[34] One will see the *centrality* of *Tifereth* in the graphic representation of the *Sephirot*, under whose *overall* (total) denomination the five peripheral spheres connected with it are sometimes also placed, thus making a total of six levels of spirituality: "The letter *vav* is the secret of the link among all the Spheres, both superior and inferior, and all of them converge in it, some of them from above and some from below, from the right and from the left, and it is this letter that bears the name of middle way" (*Sha'aré Orah*, p. 89). "In the median axis resides the secret of the letter *vav* of the Tetragrammaton, the setting in place of the Name, whose image is that of a vertical line; like this letter, this Name extends up toward infinity . . . then downward . . . and toward the sides" (*Sha'aré Orah*, p. 120). Reinserted into language, the letter *vav* leads to the verb *PshT*, which signifies "discovery," "laying bare," and "extension"—of the line—(to infinity).

In turn, the number 12 determines other symbols, signifieds that are grouped around a semantic trait "12" or linguistic signifiers the sum of whose letters adds up to the numerical value 12 (*gematria*). Among these signifiers is *zeh*, formed by the letters (z = 7) and (h = 5) (*Pardes Rimonim, Kehilath Ya'akov*).

Underlying all these configurations, the reader will have discerned a general masculine symbolics that repeats the theme of unveiling and the straight line and determines many of the associations derived from it (circumcision, the rite of pilgrimage, etc.). This symbolics serves at the same time as a vehicle for the image of the energetic, fecund influx transmitted from sphere to sphere as far as the final *Sephirah* of *Malkhuth*.

Here then is a preliminary recapitulating schema of these data.[35]

THE THEMATICS OF *Zot*

In the linguistic coherence of the Kabbalah, the demonstrative *zot* corresponds, in a specific if not univocal manner,[36] to the last of the spheres constituting the universe, that of kingdom (*Malkhuth*). Here again, as in the case of *zeh*, the core of signification multiplies into several fragments, which are the levels of being and the complementary modes of revelation of a single spiritual entity. The value designated by *zot* is refracted into different exponents of a single semantic paradigm.

The lowest of the spheres in their vertical organization, *Malkhuth* is first represented as a *receptacle*. (See p. 78.) "This Name [corresponding to *Malkhuth*] is the image of a reservoir and a receptacle" (*Sha'aré Orah*, p. 10). By definition, *Malkhuth* is primarily a *place*, that of Presence. It is the container within which the Name resides, which allows the revelation to manifest itself. The symbolic associations of this primary identification are multiple and almost obvious.[37]

Let us note here the lines of force in this thematic field, feminine in modality, which lead from woman to beauty, from water to fecundity, from the Mosaic revelation to the community

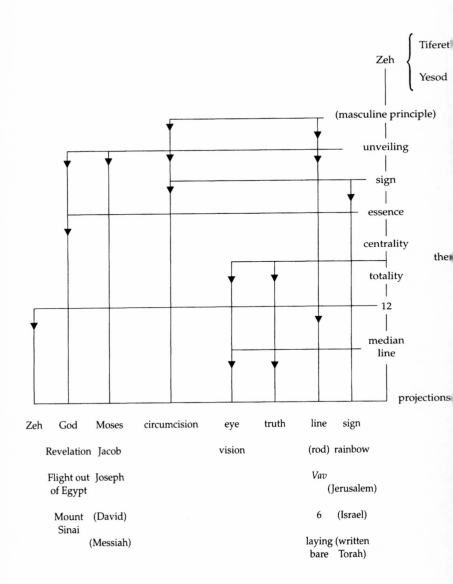

Note: Parentheses indicate the most frequent references.

of Israel. After *zeh* and in its turn, *zot* refers through a concept or a form to an event, to an experience, but also to a matter, an identity, a letter; true and authenticated in each of its possibilities, all oriented toward this same notion of a *container* in which what makes up the essence of a world is deposited (and bears fruit).

Since *zot* represents this path open in the world to the presence of God, this availability of the world to receiving the Lord's crown, it is also connected, in correlation with *Malkhuth,* with the (first) *Sephirah* of *Keter,* or Crown, which is also situated on the median axis—but at the other end of the series. However, the feminine character attached to *zot* and its value as a "recipient" give it a spatial extension and a temporal support. Its figure is the curve, its rhythm that of the number 7, the cycle of creation.[38]

Malkhuth thus represents both the possibility of Presence and Presence itself. Its thematic projections are grouped under three main rubrics, that of Presence-Providence, that of the place (sign) of presence, and that of the blessing (fecundity) through which Presence finds its place.

The Blessing (Fecundity)

As the possible principle of a land touched by Presence, *Malkhuth* receives the effluvium of the superior spheres and, according to the cycle of fecundity, showers the *blessing* "on all the creatures": "Given that the Lord spreads all profusion in the Name *Adonai*[39] [corresponding to *Malkhuth*], that the hidden treasures of the King are concealed within it, and that starting out from it they expand to satisfy the need of all creatures, the Torah refers to this Name by the designation of the blessing (*Berakhah*)" (*Sha'aré Orah,* p. 9).

A source of absolute plenitude, *Malkhuth* is also recognized as a totality: "And sometimes the name *Adonai* (*Malkhuth*) receives the denomination *kol* (all), in that it is perfection. Since all emanation, all abundance of life are contained within it, it is called 'all' because all is in it" (*Sha'aré Orah,* p. 13). This aptitude for receiving and giving, this act of maturation, is the action par excellence of the matrix, preparing its fruit.

We shall therefore emphasize the symbolic projections of woman, water, (beauty) manifested in the created world: "This sphere (*Malkhuth*) designated by *zot*, is called *Ishah*, 'woman,' according to the allusion in the verse 'This one (*zot*) shall be called woman' (Gen. 2:23) [or '*zot* will be called woman']" (*Zohar* B 37b or *Bo* 33, 112). The list of semantic equivalence projected by *Sha'aré Orah* gives, moreover, for *Malkhuth* "girl/daughter"—"woman"—"Rachel" (p. 33), whereas Rabbi Moshe Cordovero adds "fiancée."

The theme of water is also yielded by the specific configuration of the container—the sea, the reservoir, or the well: "And sometimes the Name *Adonai* is rendered by the term 'sea,' which designates the gathering of waters" (*Sha'aré Orah*, p. 12). "And this Name is in the image of a *reservoir* into which the river flows, and from which one draws enough water to irrigate the Garden and satisfy all thirst" (*Sha'aré Orah*, p. 9).[40]

In the religious order, it is the Torah that conveys and represents the principle of all blessing. The grid of kabbalistic decoding identifies *Malkhuth* as the *Oral Law* (in that it serves as a container for the Written Law)[41] (*Sha'aré Orah*, p. 28).

Finally, in the development of human history, the blessing is given to the patriarchs: "It is by this Name (*Adonai*) received as a heritage from our father Isaac, and by Isaac from Abraham, that our father Jacob blessed his children. Now the Lord blessed-be-He had told Abraham this Name in order to open to him the doors of *Adonai*, so that through this blessing he might satisfy his expectation and that of all men; and that is the profound meaning of the verse: 'And I will bless you; I will make your name great, and you shall be a blessing' (Gen. 12:2)" (*Sha'aré Orah*, p. 9).[42]

The Land is what was promised the patriarchs.

The Place (Sign) of Presence

This second thematic subdivision brings together in time and space the points available to Presence, which seeks a site in the world, a "sign-bearer."

The radiation of this Presence reaches the *Land of Israel,* and, within Israel, *Jerusalem* and its *Temple*: "Through it (*Malkhuth*)—since it resides on earth—the Israelites deserved to inherit the land, as it is said in the verse 'This (*zot*) land shall fall to you as your portion' (Num. 34:2)" (*Sha'aré Orah,* p. 28). "And the attribute corresponding to the name *Adonai* is sometimes rendered by the expression 'the house of the Temple,' because it is 'the place where the specific Name resides'" (*Sha'aré Orah,* p. 14).[43] On the scale of eternity, the Kabbalah will translate the blessing of the earth into the heritage of Eden (= the world to come).

At the heart of the nations, the sign of Presence is borne by the *community of Israel*:[44] "'My place of everlasting repose will be there' (*zot*) (Ps. 132:14): Rabbi Hizkiah taught: This proposition is uttered by the Holy One, blessed-be-He concerning the community of Israel, when Israel does His Will. For then the Holy One, blessed-be-He sits on the throne of His Glory, He extends His mercy to the world, and His blessing of love and peace. Then He can say: *zot* is my place of everlasting repose [=the foundation on which I rest]" (Zohar B 222b or *Pekudé* 16, 43).

In the chapter *Malkhuth,* the *Sha'aré Orah* also proposes, in its nomenclature, the "community of Israel" as one of the possible semantic actualizations of the name Adonaï: "It is because it has received this attribute [of *Malkhuth*] as its portion that Israel has become portion and heritage of the Lord" (*Sha'aré Orah,* p. 28).

David, of the tribe of Judah, is the particular shape taken by this kingdom over Israel. Spread over the world in *zot,* it manifests this royal sphere.

In the graphic order, the design of the ordering of the spheres, which places *Malkhuth* at the bottom of the scale, visually reproduces the structure of a basin.

Its letter is also the *last* one of the Name, or ה, with a numerical value of 5, concave in shape, according to the geometrical line that corresponds to it, and which is that of the *curve*. It prepares a space and curves inward to receive.

Presence—Providence

As the place of Presence, the *Sephirah* of *Malkhuth* ultimately refers, by a sort of metonymy, to Presence itself or *Shekhinah* (literally, "the one [feminine] who resides"). "This attribute is sometimes called *Shekhinah*, Presence, according to the terms of the verse: 'And let them make Me a sanctuary that I may *dwell* [*veshakhanti*] among them' (Exod. 25:8)" (*Sha'aré Orah*, p. 15). The Zohar corroborates this identification through several midrashim, all based on the same fundamental equation: "*zot* represents the *Shekhinah*" (Zohar C 297b, or *Ha'azinu* 95, 216).

In the existential and no longer metaphysical order, this Presence is Providence, a power both sovereign and retributive:[45] "And this *Sephirah* is named *Malkhuth* (Kingdom) because it reigns over all creatures" (*Sha'aré Orah*, p. 21). "By this attribute, I have saved you [in Egypt], and by it I shall judge you" (*Sha'aré Orah*, p. 21).

For the present study, the many-branched thematic complex of *Malkhuth*, the sphere of the container, the receptacle-sphere, is restricted to the following table (see p. 83).

Zeh AND *Zot*, THE SYMBOLICS OF UNION (→ zu)[46]

The thematics retained by the Kabbalah does not stop at the dichotomous distinction of the two spheres *Yesod* (*Tifereth*) and *Malkhuth* (*Keter*). It ends up in an independent symbolics turning on the joining of these two principles, one of them masculine, designated by *zeh*, the other feminine, subtended by *zot*, and these appear as gender variations of the same fundamental category, the modality of *revelation*. Each thematic whole acquires its full signification only in its necessary encounter with its complementary facet: "Everything happens on a single level, and the two values are not dissociated. . . . For the *covenant* represents the sphere of *Yesod*, called *zeh*, and the sphere of *Malkhuth* receives *the name of zot only at the time of its union* with the covenant, at a single level" (Zohar A 93b or *Lekh Lekha* 132, 400).

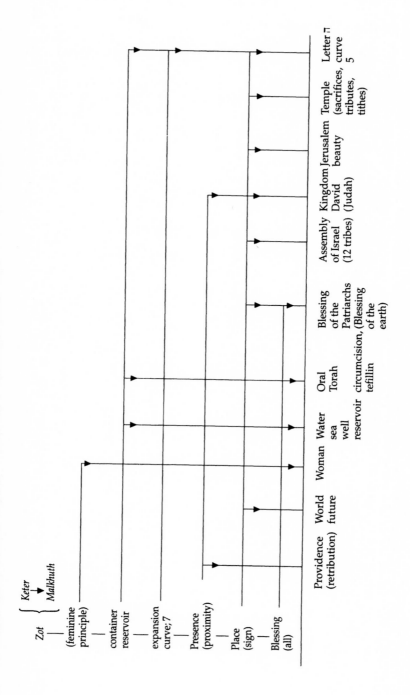

Moreover, it will have been noted in the preceding tables that *zeh* and *zot* designate exclusively the spheres situated directly on the median axis. On the latter is played out, through differing harmonics, the fundamental problematics of unity. In its centrality, it in fact simultaneously provides a focal point for the symbolics of *union* and *unveiling*: vertically, it is the site of the linking of the superior and inferior *Sephiroth*. This new harmony is developed for itself, but it rapidly appears that it extends the thematic coherence of the spheres that compose it and is inscribed in their wake.

Centrality (Synthesis)

Vertically, the median axis actualizes the *synthesis* of the lateral values (it thus guarantees at the same time a direct, *immediate* relation between the superior and inferior spheres; see below): "You shall find that the Name of the Lord, which represents the secret of the median way, dwells in the middle" (*Sha'aré Orah*, p. 114). Whence a thematics of the center, attached to the spheres borne by this axis: "Three entities are grouped *at the center*: the Name of the Lord on top, surrounded by all the Princes, . . . Israel on the bottom, *in the middle*, surrounded by all the peoples, and finally Jerusalem, the heritage of the Lord, which represents the land of Israel, encircled on all sides by the territories of the other peoples, according to the terms of the verse: 'Here is [*zot*] Jerusalem in the middle of the nations' (Ezek. 5:5)" (*Sha'aré Orah*, p. 99).

Unveiling

This centrality is symbolized in unveiling, in its graphic, metaphysical, moral, sexual plurivalence:

> But when the Lord blessed-be-He unites with the just and fervent, the pillars of the world, then He puts off His surnames and His Name alone is raised up, and then He is intimate with Israel, like a king who has taken off his robes and unites with his wife. That is the hidden meaning of the verse: "Return, rebellious children, says the Lord, I want to make a covenant with

you" (Jer. 3:14). And the text further says: "Then I will betroth you to me for eternity" (Hos. 2:21). And that is the deep meaning of the verse: "I have taken off my tunic, how could I put it on again?" (Song of Sol. 5:3).

(*Sha'aré Orah*, p. 97)

By a metaphorical shift, the axis of the unveiling becomes the space of the *revelation*, in which God, lifting "his veils, does away with the intermediaries" (*Sha'aré Orah*, p. 102).

Union

This laying bare, a prelude to knowledge, makes union possible. The latter is realized, borne by the median axis, at any of its points. In fact: "Each of the degrees of the Name is composed of two principles, one active, the other passive" (*Sha'aré Orah*, p. 115).

This dialectic of the recipient and the gift, recognized as what is at stake in the relation between the creature and the Creator, is extended to the universal, "in each of its degrees" on the vertical scale of the median axis, through the generic distinction between the masculine and the feminine. It will thus be understood that the last two spheres, designated respectively by *zeh* and *zot*, see their cohesion expressed in the form of mystical weddings: "'This one (*Zot*) this time is bone of my bone, and flesh of my flesh' (Gen. 2:23): this designation is that of the *Shekhinah* or 'Providence,' the 'young fiancée' of the median line (*zeh*). It is said concerning it, *zot hapaam*, 'this one this time,' I know then that it is indeed bone of my bone, flesh of my flesh. That is, Providence, before its union with the superior Spheres, is still called 'the young fiancée,' and only later deserves the name of *Ishah*, 'woman'" (Zohar A 28a or Gen. 235, 282).

This nuptial motif may also have particular semantic determinations: in the encounter of the spheres of *Yesod* (*zeh*) and *Malkhuth* (*zot*), the Zohar tells us, it is the *Community of Israel* (called *zot*, i.e., *Malkhuth*) that unites with the Name, and it is *Moses* (designated by *zeh*) who unites with Providence (Zohar C 115b or *Behukotai* 18, 56, and Zohar C 148a or *Naso* 221, 193).

The Temple is the privileged site where the contraries unite, a prefiguration of the unity realized in the superior spheres. Within its enclosure, figuring on earth the celestial dwelling, the antagonisms of the natural world are reconciled.[47]

This thematics of harmony will be developed in the exposition of the whole given by the rabbi Elie Munk, on the basis of a kabbalistic exegesis. Concerning the verse: "If a man marries his sister . . ." (Lev. 20:17):

> The system of the *Sephiroth* describes the universe for us in the form of a pyramid. At the apex, which is situated in the metaphysical spheres, the absolute unity of all the elements of creation reigns; mind and matter, love and justice, form and content are one. The base is constituted by the material world in which dualism, the antagonisms and the multiplicity of the elements reign. It is for men to restore the unity of the diverse elements, but this unity remains relative; it cannot attain the absolute, which exists only at the apex and which is surrounded by the divine mystery.
>
> Now the union of the sexes represents a distant reflection of the union of the elements prefigured in the cosmological order. (These elements are also placed under the sign of the masculine and the feminine, the former represented by the fertilizing factors, the source of energy, and the latter by the receptive factors, agents of the form.) But it is limited in its essence. It cannot go as far as the amalgam that embraces all the elements, from the most heterogeneous to the most homogenous, for total integration exists only at the apex, in the absolute unity of the metaphysical spheres.[48]

This absolute unity is represented in the Jewish symbolics by the prime number 13, according to the unveiled number of the thirteen attributes of God. This number corresponds at the same time to the numeric transcription of the word "One," EHaD—[1 + 8 + 4]—and, by arithmetical derivation, to that of the Name of God, with a value of 26 (*Kehilath Ya'akov*).

The Covenant

Integration is not identity. The first principle is that of fecundation, the other of fecundity; one a principle of form, the other of substance. The conjunction of these two elements is presented in the dissymmetrical mode of the intrusion, the penetration, the *spilling-over* of the one into the other. "Thus the Name *Adonai*,[49] like a basin into which all blessings spill over, comes from the word *adonim*, the pedestals of the court in which the columns are embedded" (*Sha'aré Orah*, p. 10). The image will be repeated by the representation of *Yesod* as "the tree of life," standing "in the middle of the Garden" (*Sha'aré Orah*, p. 120).

We have defined this dialectic of a tendency to give and an aptitude to receive as the intersection of the straight line and the curve, in the module of the impossible that is the symbol ח. At the intersection of the limit and the infinite, the order of the limit marks the reality of the recipient, and the order of the infinite marks the effluvium that pours forth in it. This point of convergence between two incommensurable immensities, between men's thirst and the innumerable waters of Providence, is designated by the complex (*zeh, zot*)—or the neuter pronoun *zou*. It affirms the metaphysical possibility of a *covenant* between the Creator and his universe, between the infinite of the celestial radiation and the limits of the receptacle's absorption.[50] On the moral level, it achieves the sanctification of the creature, conceived as an inalienable presence of the spiritual in human nature, as a spiritual trace in Nature, the emergence, the unveiling of the superior sphere in the inferior sphere.

Even in the intimacy of the flesh, this trace is manifested by *circumcision*. In cosmic time, it is manifested by the Sabbath, and in history, by peace (*Sha'aré Orah*, p. 41). Under the entry "*zeh*" of its dictionary, the *Pardes Rimonim* brings together these different perspectives (on the basis of the Zohar):

And one finds in the Zohar [B 236b, or *Pekudé*, 100, 308], a teaching of Rabbi Shimeon Bar Yohai: Why is *Kedushah* (holiness) designated by *zeh* and *zot*? It is because it is in constant symbiosis with man, in the secret of the *covenant*. Here are the terms of the Zohar: "The spirit of holiness is called *zot*, because the covenant is a *holy inscription*, always engraved on man"; and it is this way that we must reread the verses: "This [*zeh*] is our God in Whom we have put our trust" (Isa. 25:3); 'This [*zeh*] is my God, I do him homage' (Exod. 15:2). Do not be astonished that *zot* is related to the Sphere of *Malkhuth*, and *zeh* to that of *Yesod* and *Tifereth*. For it is these three Spheres *as a whole* that

> are called the covenant, and which, in truth, are connected with
> the secret of circumcision. . . . And since the body and the cov-
> enant are considered as one, all three are presented in man for-
> ever, in the secret of the covenant. That is why these Spheres
> are named through a term of presence, as if one were pointing
> to them with one's finger: *"zeh."*
>
> (*Pardes Rimonim, Sha'ar Erké Hakinuyim, zeh*)

Under the generic qualifier of holiness, *Pardes Rimonim* brings
together here three dimensions of the semantic field of (*zeh, zot*)
at this higher level of signification: insofar as it is the specific
term designating *Kedushah, zeh* is coextensive with the idea of
peace (compatibility of contraries), of the trace (or point of intersection between incommensurable magnitudes), and of Presence
(the permanence of the symbiosis).

It is this point of tangency that ultimately constitutes the specific reference of the demonstrative as such (see p. 89).

This third panel of the thematic organization of the spheres
designated by the demonstrative, which goes beyond the duality of gender, seems to repeat many elements that were earlier
divided between the two groups, in particular the notions of
"presence" (*zot*) and "unveiling" (*zeh*). Nevertheless a new thematic exponent is added here, the *union of contraries*, which
makes the covenant possible. The covenant unveils the very
principle of a Presence *in* the world and its ontological possibility.

CATEGORIAL SHIFTS

These intersections and returns have at the same time another
raison d'être. In fact, these superimpositions of one table on
the other, this uncertainty in the thematic classification of the
spheres, these spillovers, and these repetitions are not the result of chance, or of a disordered amalgamation. Rather, what
they betray on the theoretical level is the imbrication of these
classes, their openness; and even more than that, the primacy
of their *deep structure*, which is reproduced at all levels of meaning, like a single chord over several octaves.

In principle, the correspondence between *Sephirah* and concept is never established term-for-term, but only grounds the

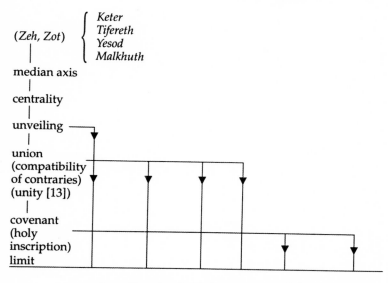

appurtenances of models, abstract figures that have been slipped one over the other, transferred from one level to another, in partial coincidences, in harmonics, in responses. The configuration of the spheres is repeated from universe to universe, and returns, as a *mise en abyme*, within each sphere itself.[51] Thus the doublet *zeh/zot* could have been recapitulated in the ambivalence of the focus and of its expansion, of the essence and the space, of the first principle and its deployment, which are refracted, repeated, and interpreted at each level of being.

The Kabbalah recognizes, as participating in its theoretical reflection itself, an impregnation of the lower levels by the upper levels, and a sort of gradual "metonymization" of all semantic categories. The *Sephirah* of *Malkhuth*, for example, takes on, in addition to its own system, the values received from the superior spheres, whose name it assimilates, in an act of opening that is simultaneously semantic (the reservoir) and functional (a sign open to several possible references).[52]

"Because of the fact that this Value [*Malkhuth*] is filled with the profusion of virtues that are superior to it [situated above it], it sometimes keeps their name, in accord with the particular virtue which invests it at a precise moment" (*Sha'aré Orah*, p. 30). This explains the repetitions we have noted, and, along with numerous similarities between the different lists drawn up by kabbalistic dictionaries, a few divergences. Thus the semantic unit "circumcision" is common—with internal modifications that make it understood in different ways—to the thematic groups of *zot*, of *zeh*, and of the pair (*zeh, zot*) (*Sha'aré Orah, Pardes Rimonim*).

Similarly, as we have seen, the Torah—in its double polarity, written and oral—is in the realm of *zeh* (*Yesod*) as well as that of *zot* (*Malkhuth*). The Sabbath also figures in (*zot*) and in (*zeh, zot*). The twelve tribes, which are normally placed along the axis of (*zot*), can be shifted toward (*zeh*). The *Kehilath Ya'akov* places David, the principle of royalty (*Malkhuth*), in *Yesod*, and the *Sefer Erké Hakinuyim* places the king-Messiah in (*zeh*).[53] The *mitzva* (or precept), which is normally feminine (*zot*), can also be integrated into (*zeh*) (*Sefer Erké Hakinuyim*).

Sometimes an association or identification can arise from an unsuspected network, from a subtler relation—within the limits of the play of meaning instituted by the tradition. For example, the *Kehilath Ya'akov*[54] cites the "angels of the Service," *malakhé hashareth*, or on the contrary, Satan and "Goliath the Philistine," negative figures, in its nomenclature of *zeh*—unusual endings that do not appear in other dictionaries consulted and which are difficult to connect, a priori at least, with the symbolic cycles proposed. In the same way, the *Sefer Erké Hakinuyim* alone gives "fire" and "rod" as equivalents of *zeh*.[55]

We will summarize these indications by observing that the Kabbalah chooses to present its semantic grids in a combination of oriented *axes*, on which the particular referential determinations *move* about as so many variables. *Zeh* and *zot*, on the median axis, can thus ultimately be located in any position whatever, in accord with a feminine/masculine division that opens to *zeh* the *Tifereth-Yesod* segment, and to *zot* the *Keter-Malkhuth* segment; through another transitivity, it makes possible the inversions of meaning and the reconstructions that ultimately emerge in a general thematics of union.[56]

This coded level, where hermeneutics finds its end, is thus not for all that an ending or a closure. The ensemble is plastic, both in its references and in the operations that make it possible to arrive at it. The analysis of these procedures leads in fact to the same indeterminacies: on the basis of distinct planes of meaning, concurrent generative techniques are superimposed and are both concordant and separated.

It remains to broaden the methodological bases.

THE CONVENTIONAL DERIVATIONS

These modes of derivation are divided according to the three fundamental registers, conventional, logical, formal, and correspond to an approximately[57] parallel subdivision of the matrix-sign into three levels of meaning, according to whether it is considered as a global sign (regulating a conventional derivation), as a signified (logical production), or as a signifier (formal production).

By definition, this matrix-sign is itself formed of an ensemble of constitutive traits, of form or of meaning, of signifiers or of signifieds, to which paradigmatic series of signs having this common trait will be attached. This construction makes it possible to turn the wheel of possible permutations on its axis and to generate the whole class on the basis of any one of its elements.

This ensemble is theoretically always self-identical (an observation that will be confirmed in the course of our study), despite the demarcations that make it branch out, and it is always based on the tradition that establishes its harmony (which the Hebrew word *kabbalah* translates quite faithfully).

THE CONVENTIONAL REGISTER

The ensemble of the synonyms or signs of a single truth, the possible "references" of a single primary "sense," is established first of all by convention, and transmitted by the cultural heritage. The list of these synonyms or signs is given—incomplete, or filled with variant, but *given*, as we know, in numerous kabbalistic lexicons.[58] In accord with the received tradition, each word of the Bible is thus inserted into some semantic context or other, in an organized cycle of ramifications.

This grounding in the wisdom of the Fathers explains certain uncertainties or ambiguities in the filiation of the themes; as in the case of talmudic disputations, the pluralism of traditions is recognized. This can be seen, for example, in the article on "*davar*," "speech" or "thing," which R. Moshe Cordovero puts in the "semantic sphere" of *Malkhuth*, while at the same time reporting other opinions that situate it in the sphere of *Yesod*.

Where the logical or linguistic justification of the teaching is concealed, the conventional nature of the decision appears all the more forcefully, based first of all on faith in a memory of reading. Thus each time *Sha'aré Orah* affirms the appurtenance of a term (and behind it, that of a concept) to a given *Sephirah* without motivating it in any way, it comes out that the reason for this mode of ordering is anchored, more deeply than the apparent explanation, "in the revelation to Moses of the Oral Law." The turns of phrase addressing the reader allude to this, by appealing to a principle of authority of the type "And know that . . . " or "As we have informed you" (p. 13), or assertive propositions such as "And everywhere where we find such-and-such an expression, such-and-such an intention of the text is revealed" (p. 122), or "And here is the secret meaning of such and such a term," or even more simply "And we have *learned* that . . . "

Above all, *Sha'aré Orah*, which starts out from the entire semantic class and not from the isolated sign, allows us to understand the term as an illustration or partial determination of the generic signified, at a particular point in the overall corpus *already* assimilated by the analysis.

THE LOGICAL REGISTER

Although this translation is hallowed by tradition and would suffice by itself, a logical justification for the relationship established is usually added to it. The various kabbalistic lexicons, through which a classification of the sacred language into ten fundamental semantic fields is sketched out, at the same time propose an organized model of conventional classification that is authorized by the tradition, as well as explicit forms of *motivation* for this classification.[59]

Considered from the point of view of its signified, the matrix-sign is at the origin of several logical series of referentialization. We will recognize, for reasons of methodological clarity, an internal division of meaning into two levels, according to whether the originary concept is of a functional (thematic) or a figurative order. In both cases, it remains a concept, and is inscribed within a framework of signification susceptible to logical argumentation.

Thematic Logic

On the basis of a fundamental *theme,* kabbalistic classification deduces associations grounded in reason; the exposition of the series is thus based on argumentation of a causal type: "And the reason for this is," "because," "that is why," and so on. Here are a few examples.

As we know, the theme of the *Sephirah* of *Malkhuth* is the idea of the receptacle. From this central structure are deduced, on homologous planes, all sorts of symbolic projections: "And the attribute corresponding to the Name *Adonai*[60] is sometimes rendered by the expression 'the house of the Temple,' *because* it is the 'dwelling where the specific Name resides'" (*Sha'aré Orah*, p. 14).

The Oral Law is identified with this same value: "*And the reason is* that the Lord's Torah, which is the Written Law, resides in this virtue, and that the Oral Law is like a tent and an arch for it" (*Sha'aré Orah*, p. 30).

But it is the image of water that is most often associated with this figure of the container: "And sometimes the Name *Adonai* is indicated in the text by the word 'sea.' The latter in fact refers to the land that holds back the water . . . hence one can say that 'sea' is the name given to the gathering of the waters" (*Sha'aré Orah*, p. 12).

"And sometimes the Name *Adonai* is designated in the Torah by the term *Be'er*, 'the well,' because it is a well filled with
water" (*Sha'aré Orah*, p. 11).

Figurative Logic

In the preceding examples, the notion of receptacle has a structural value and generates functionally analogous objects. But
beyond its conceptual definition the theme of each *Sephirah* also
assumes a material image: that of the reservoir (of the curve)
or that of the straight line. This register develops in turn a motivated series of signs, whose logical principle is a common
configuration.

If these two semantic levels, one a level of functioning and
the other a level of concretization, more or less coincide in the
symbols they evoke with regard to the unit (*zot*) (design or
principle of the reservoir), in *(zeh)* they diverge more clearly.
The optical image of unveiling, which corresponds to the sphere
of *Yesod*, is rendered, according to the Kabbalah, by a median
line linking the upper and lower worlds, the "right-hand" virtues and the "left-hand" virtues. This line in turn secretes a
group of "formally" comparable representations. Its letter will
be the letter ו (*vav*), the third letter of the Tetragrammaton, represented in writing by a *vertical line*.[61] Parallel to the class of
the *"signs"* of revelation we will thus find a class of *linear* objects all oriented toward the same preliminary axis (for example, Moses' rod).

THE FORMAL REGISTER

Finally, material image and thematic function are both rendered by one or several keywords that serve as their support.[62]
This signifying level calls for two types of derivation.

Signified Level

The first type of derivation, which is connected with the signified traits inscribed in the signifier, produces as before a log-

ical series with a formal semantic basis. It is in particular the principle of the functioning of *gematria*, which calculates the numerical value of a term on the basis of the sum of its letters. This is an arithmetical operation that is quickly semanticized in a general symbolics of numbers: if *zeh*, with a numerical equivalent of 12, can be in its turn designated as the primary signifier, it will entail the determination of a series of derived terms on the *thematic* base 12.[63] This numerically coded relay, deduced from a signifier, takes on a semantic value to reproduce an associative series of signifieds: thus the 12 months of the year, the 12 signs of the Zodiac, the 12 fundamental letters defining the 12 dimensions of the celestial chariot (*Sha'aré Orah*, p. 137).

Similarly, Jacob, by way of his twelve sons: "And just as the name of the Lord, blessed-be-He is situated in the center, and all the qualifiers are linked with him all around him, in the same way Jacob, identified with the twelve tribes that represent the secret of the twelve dimensions of the universe, is linked to the name of the Lord, blessed-be-He" (*Sha'aré Orah*, p. 129).

Indirect elements of signification are in fact mixed into the process of classification by twelve: it is by way of the detour through his descendants that Jacob is identified with the number 12, and by a cultural convention that the months of the year are twelve in number.[64]

Signifier Level

The only properly formal derivation articulated on the signifier is lexical variation that is spun out starting from an initial lexeme. These paradigms have no law of associativity other than that of a morphological or phonological shift internal to language that exploits the consonantal structure of Hebrew. Thus from *berekhah*, "reservoir," can be generated by way of the signifier the terms *berakhah*, "blessing," and *bekhora*, "birthright" (*Sha'aré Orah*, p. 10). *Zakhar*, the masculine principle (*Yesod*) (*Pardes Rimonim*), is associated with *zekher* (*zikaron*) "memory" (*Sha'aré Orah*, p. 41), *lakhem*, "for you," turns into "*melekh*, 'king' (connected with *Malkhuth*, the sphere of 'royalty')" (*Sefer Erké Hakinuyim*, entry *zeh* [Torah]).[65]

It will be observed that it is on the basis of the signifier, and through the mechanism of formal operations, that combinations of letters and numbers, new constellations of terms, gravitate around a given term, in a kind of acrostic play. At this level, the algorithm of gematria becomes far more complex; it embeds in words the *name* itself (along with the associated numeric value) of the letters that form them (*bemilui*); the semantic content of the numbers it draws off no longer appears directly[66] and is absorbed into a pure calculus of equivalence between signifiers.[67]

This presentation, whose levels can be summarized by the following table, does not exhaust the modes of formation of the semantic paradigms in the Kabbalah.[68] Numerous combinations are difficult to classify because of their mixed nature.

Levels of Signification		Types of Derivation
Sign		conventional
Signified	function (theme)	logical
	figure	
Signifier	numerical value	logical
	lexeme	formal
	literality	

What we must remember from these oppositions is that the Sod level of interpretation discovers, at the same time as certain glosses concealed up to that point, unusual modes of meaning's functioning.

The generating principle of each sphere, taken each time in a different register, produces, on the basis of the traits of sense (or of form) that compose it, parallel axes of derivation that eventuate in a multitude of symbolic determinations that can be represented by the schema below.

Initial Sign Sign	Derived Reference Reference
a (sign)	a'
b (signified: theme)	b'
c (signified: form).............................	c'
d (signifier: word).............................	d'
e (signifier: letters, numbers)...........	e'
f...	f'
g	g'

Most of the time, the relation established associates sign "a" with reference "a'," sign "b" with reference "b'," and so on. But this correspondence is far from imperative, and crossings, buds, and grafts constantly appear.

In particular, a principle of the union of contraries that finds here its mode of expression on the *functional* level is confirmed. The great surprise of this level of exegesis, in fact, is that it reconciles heterogeneous derivations and at least partially blends their endings. The spectra of signs appear very near to each other and always come back to the same harmonies. To take only one example, the complex *berakhah-berekha-bekhorah* (reservoir-blessing-birthright) is presented simultaneously as a thematic series (in the coherence of the Bible, the *reservoir* is a figure of the *blessing,* and the blessing—of the Land— is the privilege of the birthright) and as a lexical series.[69] The Kabbalah posits, without explicitly recognizing them (so natural to it are these shifts in tone, these chromaticisms), a compatibility and complementarity of registers and relations that modern consciousness disassociates.

Thus we can return to the different tables inscribed in this chapter, which proposed a group of thematic projections of the demonstrative, and recognize in them at the same time a synoptic—though incomplete—inventory of the possible anagogic references of *zeh,* in any of the deductive series of derivation in which they may be involved. Whatever the path taken by the analysis—whatever methodological path, that is, taking into account at the same time the mobility of the series—it ultimately ends up in the same ramifications.

In each of its faces, its unveilings, the same value carries to the extreme the development of its symbols, which all end up, at some point in their "expansion," intersecting with each other, meeting each other, coming together. That is why each class of equivalence can be detected through the letters, forms, grammatical meanings, thematic symbolizations: the line always comes back to the unveiling, the letter always makes six, the Name is always situated at the center of experience.

Simultaneously, although the theoretical foundations of the phenomenon are not yet clarified, an interpenetration of the categories and functionings of meaning (in particular of the signifying and signified levels of the sign and of the associative mechanisms that are specific to them) that grows continually deeper is also posited. The following chapters will have to plumb the depths of this interpenetration.

4

Thematic Convergence

The level of the interpretation of Sod was presented as radically discontinuous with respect to the lower levels of exegesis. This discontinuity makes itself felt even at these first levels, since the analysis, which is centered first on the sense of the demonstrative (and its fixation in language) and then on its references in discourse, is split into divergent approaches.

In this chapter I intend to restore to the broken line of exegesis a continuity that is first of all thematic, by juxtaposing the specific semanticizations at which these superimposed procedures arrive. There is a surprising convergence of the results obtained at the first stages of commentary, in the direction of a semantic horizon line that would be that of Sod.

In other words, the anagogic level of interpretation is presented as the demonstrative's ultimate place of reference, the backdrop of the first registers of exegesis, whose choices it conditions and whose connotations it regulates. At the end of the hermeneutic path, the same signs are still repeated; that is, the same references are selected, pivoting around the same axes of signification.

Understood in this way, the anagogic level and its conventional paradigms appear to coincide with the subterranean code discerned earlier, which somewhat disoriented the regular linguistic functioning of the demonstrative in the examination of the commentary.

We recall in fact that the stages of a "double articulation" of exegesis were posited as early as its "immediate" level, since the sense of the demonstrative seemed to be based on an internal regulation of another order (the level of parasitic signification indicated as S2),[1] whereas this same regularity emerged again, mutatis mutandis, on the level of speech, and of the references *in praesentia* that the latter made it possible to recognize.

This recurrence in the referentialization was moving in the direction of an organized thematic structure, indicated as R2.[2]

What the comparison of the results obtained in each register tends to show is that these secondary levels of signification, S2 and R2, levels secretly connoted by exegesis, in which both the senses and the references of the demonstrative are determined by the traditional coherence, coincide with the generic signified proposed by Sod and with the references attached to it. The massive character of the correspondences noted and their systematic inscription within one or another of the spheres of signification defined by Sod confirm this hypothesis.

It will be recognized that the level of Sod is thus indeed the locus of all the possible interpretations, the axis of coordinates in relation to which every punctual attempt to find a signification, every elucidation of a reference, is situated.

For methodological reasons, we shall distinguish first a relation between sense and sense, indicated as S1 → S2, that bridges the gap between the semantic givens of chapter 1, which was devoted to the study of the "senses" of *zeh* (Peshat, Derash), and the fundamental traits of the *Sephiroth* respectively associated with *zeh* by anagogic reading.[3]

A second relation establishes a correspondence between the referentializations of *zeh* in context, displayed in chapter 2 (Remez, Derash), and the thematic constellations[4] derived by Sod from the kernel of sense of each *Sephirah* (R1 → R2). In this case as in the other, the elements of signification, whose superimposition is made possible by the homogeneous—semiotic[5]—character of the ramifications envisaged, are reflected or repeated.[6] However, the demonstrative will be confronted by more ambiguous examples, which oscillate between determination by the text and a semantics of reading.

FROM DEMONSTRATIVE MEANING TO
ANAGOGIC MEANING: S1 → S2

We underscored, in examining the senses of *zeh* (based on a literal or parabolic reading), a tendency to a thematization of the instructions linked with the demonstrative in the linguistic

system.[7] This thematization is inserted into a general disequi-
librium of the relations of determination, reinforcing the deictic in relation to its context. This first step toward a deeper thematization endowed the contexts encountered with a sememe
of (a) "restriction" (specificity, uniqueness) and (b) "presence"
(proximity, concretization)—sometimes itself extrapolated into
"recognition" or "visualization."

If we recognize in addition, as the global signified of *zeh* on
the anagogic level, an original concept of *representation*, the unveiling of the infinite in the concrete, a homology of the mi-
crocosm and the macrocosm, which is the organization in the
real, perceptible by man, of the principle of his spiritual viabil-
ity—then we will acknowledge the concord of this notion with
the *thematic radicalization of the grammatical sense of zeh.*

In this reading, the thematization of the demonstrative function is integrated into an interpretation seeing *Yesod* (*Tifereth*)
and *Malkhuth* as the spheres of the "presence" of God in the
world.[8] In the experience of the Revelation the mark of a *nearby*
Providence and the perception of its *uniqueness* are merged in
the *visible* point in time and space where the Kabbalah recognizes the immediate *sign* of a beyond.

One also finds the genre distinction transposed into the opposition between two principles of the universe, masculine and
feminine. Whereas *zeh*, the masculine, represents the source of
energy, the form *zot* evokes the receptacle of fecundity. On this
basis, the constellation of *Malkhuth* allows new "referential"
points, alternately woman and water, Israel as land and as fiancée; whereas *Yesod* unveils a saving God, the life-giving flux
of His will.[9]

It is obviously no accident that the demonstrative (whose
grammatical sense authorizes it to designate a present and
nearby object that is recognizable more than known, in an existential relation with the subject but *indefinite* as to its nature)
refers at the same time, in the configuration of the spheres it
designates, to the double experience of Providence and Revelation, which is a double mystery.

The relation of the sense of *zeh* in the linguistic system to the
sense defined by Sod can be said to be one of homology.[10] More

Homologous Signifieds on the S1 and S2 Levels

	Sepharah	Yesod	Malkhuth	Yesod / Malkhuth
transiction (textualization)	generic theme of the sphere	Revelation (median axis)	Presence	Revelation Presence
	thematization of sense traits	uniqueness specificity	concretization visualization	knowledge (proximity) recognition
S1	gender	masculine	feminine	neuter (masculine and feminine)
linguistic level	semantic function	demonstrative function (designation)		deictic function (localization)

precisely, the generic signified of (*zeh, zot*) at a coded level of reading appears as the ultimate *thematization* of the grammatical traits of the demonstrative. Unveiled at its root as early as the parabolic treatment of the Midrash, this thematization went along with an autonomization of the demonstrative function in which we have perceived the laws of superadded senses exterior to the linguistic circuit proper.

The details of the semantic determinations advanced by midrash in the framework of these transfers of sense, and more particularly of the effects of thematization, has not been analyzed in a systematic manner. One can nevertheless imagine at least a partial integration of these themes in Sod's grids.

For example, the examination of certain midrashim of "visualization"[11]—selected arbitrarily—yields the following correspondences:

zeh	lampstand	*Yesod*
zeh	moon	*Yesod*
zeh	animal	*Malkhuth*
zeh	Jacob	*Tifereth*
zeh	Moses	*Tifereth*

FROM CONTEXTUAL REFERENCES TO CODED REFERENCES: R1 → R2

It will be still more easily seen that the class of R1 references[12] (tracked in the biblical text by the Derash or the Remez and organized into an underlying thematic structure through successive connotations) can be assimilated to the referential series Sod derives from each *Sephirah*. In fact, if one reconsiders all the results of the contextual semanticizations proposed in chapter 2, it will be found that they are all[13] inscribed in the table of the anagogic classes of equivalence centered on *zeh* (*Tifereth, Yesod*) or on *zot* (*Malkhuth*).

Hence, parallel to the relation [(grammatical sense)→(anagogic sense)] we will recognize a relation [(textual references)→ (coded references)] that tends to superimpose the disparate data of the textualization and the structured paradigm of Sod. This convergence was once again begun, or at least prepared for, by the systematic return of the same themes in the first stages of the examination of the contexts, through which, beyond individual cases, a new order of sense was revealed. These propositions can be verified in the following schema, which sums up and organizes the results obtained in chapter 2.

For *zeh*:

	Contextual references
• "This is my God" (*Menahoth* 53b)	→ *God*
• "What use to me is the birthright?" (*Midrash Rabbah*, Gen. 68:13)	→ *God*
• "This month will be for you" (*Sanhedrin* 42a)	→ *God*
• "This Book of the Torah" (*Sefer Erké Hakinuyim*)	→ *Torah*
• "That is man" (*Sefer Erké Hakinuyim*)	→ *Commandment (mitzva)*
• "This is the thing" (*Midrash Rabbah*, Num. 12:8)	→ *Circumcision*
• "Go this way" (Rabbi Bahyé, Exod. 19:24)	→ *Rod*
• "This is how you shall proceed" (*Midrash Rabbah*, Exod. 38:8)	→ *Israel (12 tribes)*
• "Here is the tribute" (*Midrash Rabbah*, Lev. 8:1)	→ *Israel (12 tribes)*
• "That man Moses" (*Menahoth* 53b)	→ *Moses*
• "They departed this place" (*Sefer Erké Hakinuyim*)	→ *Joseph*

For *Zot*:

	Contextual references
• "In 'this' I have confidence" (*Midrash Rabbah*, Lev. 21:2)	→ *Torah* *Judah (royalty)*
• "And this is the Torah" (*Avodah Zarah* 2b)	→ *Torah*
• "Here is the rule" (Rabbi Bahyé, *Vayehi*)	→ *Torah*

		Contextual references
• "This is how Aaron shall enter" (*Midrash Rabbah*, Lev. 21:6)		→ *Torah* *Circumcision (covenant)* *Chabbat (covenant)* *Jerusalem* *Tribes (Israel)* *Judah (royalty)* *Community of Israel*
	Temple (covenant)	*Terumah* *Tithes* *Offerings*
• "This came to us from the Lord" (*Yalkut Shimoni* II, 876)		→ *Community of Israel*
• "This is the blessing" (*Sifré,* Deut. 392 L 17; *Devarim Rabbah,* 4, 4)		→ *Blessing of the Patriarchs*
• "This is the sign of the covenant" (*Sefer Erké Hakinuyim, Zeh*)		→ *Rainbow*
• "This is the covenant" (*Midrash Rabbah,* Exod. 23:12)		→ *Circumcision*

This superimposition shows quite clearly that the two levels of exegesis, which are apparently heterogeneous in method, converge in their contents. This superimposition allows us to read the thematic code identified on the plane of Sod in the spectrum of each *Sephirah* as the secret, generic *axis* of the punctual references advanced by the different commentaries.

However, this division between traits of the linguistic system and specific speech acts does not suffice to explain the referential determinations obtained, and governs them only in part, in the "pure" examples of thematization and intertextuality. If in fact we recognize in most midrashim a systematics based on a characteristic textual *signal*, the latter does not claim to justify the choice of a particular semanticization.

This factor of homogeneity seems, moreover, to grow weaker

as the commentary disengages itself from the norms of demonstrative sense or from the conditioning of contextual memory. New examples load the occurrence of the pronoun *zeh* with new significations that are discontinuous with respect to its traditional rules of use.

We will admit in general that Midrash's propositions, which are sometimes broadened into complete thematic cycles, are not foreseeable through the (intratextual) play of language alone: neither the sense of the demonstrative nor its references in discourse can suffice to calculate its parabolic extension. In particular, one cannot eliminate, in any theory of exegesis, a variable parameter of exegesis, which reintegrates into the message a problematics of the subject and of reception: Midrash in fact acknowledges, as a technique of interpretation, the projection of the biblical model onto various planes of existential actualization. To the extent to which these interpretations appear arbitrary—a spontaneous diagnostics made by a temperament or a period—they seem irreducible to analysis, understood as a necessary law of signification, and, because of their indeterminacy, difficult to systematize into structured semantic fields. Thus moral considerations, existential responses, pertain to an independent ideology that flows along with history and produces its own myths.[14]

We shall propose the hypothesis that even these chance recognitions of a theme (more or less based on the value of *zeh*, into which a new sensibility inserts its contingent inspiration, without recognizing the textual limit of any approach), even these thematic traces themselves, are inscribed in turn within networks prepared by convention, in the immense referential wheel of the possible projections of the demonstrative.[15]

We shall illustrate this thesis in two main phases. The first will examine the thematic extensions derived from a rigorous hermeneutic framework, but whose logic is to be sought beyond the obvious features of the text. In the second phase, the examples show themselves more freely homiletic, grafted onto the narrative as foreign buds, and no longer regulated by its imperatives.[16] The exact proportion of these phenomena within each midrash is difficult to determine; it remains significant by its very presence, and its principle is confirmed by traditional exegesis.[17]

SEMANTICIZATIONS DERIVED
FROM THE SENSE

"When she opened it, she saw that it was a child, a boy crying. She took pity on it and said, 'This (*zeh*) must be a Hebrew child'" (Exod. 2:6). The Midrashic commentary: "And she said: 'This must be a Hebrew child.' How did she recognize it? Rabbi Yossé ben Rabbi Hanina teaches: because she saw that it was circumcised" (*Midrash Rabbah*, Exod. 1:24).

We recall that certain midrashim on this same verse exhausted through their interpretation the semantic trait of "restriction" or "proximity" (see chap. 1, p. 28). The commentary presented here is based on the function of *recognition* attached *to the use of zeh* by Peshat. However, its limits are exceeded by the specific theme chosen: a conventional line passes implicitly from "circumcision" through the character of "Moses" and the demonstrative "*zeh*" as far as the totalizing sphere of *Tifereth*, which includes these diverse signifieds within its paradigm.[18]

In a second example—Moses' prayer to God when he is stopped at the gates of the Holy Land—the midrash thematizes the sememe of *proximity*: "Let me, I pray, cross over and see the good land on the other side of the Jordan, that good hill, and the Lebanon" (Deut. 3:25). "That good hill: this refers to Jerusalem" (*Berakhoth* 48b). To be sure, Moses could pray for no other hill than that of the Temple. At the same time that it plumbs Moses' heart—a desire for spirituality and not a pure desire for survival—the Midrash establishes (unveils) a precise system of correlations: "*zeh*," "good," and "hill" are set alongside each other in a single semantic series based on *Yesod*, to which "Jerusalem" (based on *Malkhuth*) is added.[19] To this "proximity" in space corresponds, in the next verse, a "temporal proximity": "Because you have done this (*zeh*) and have not withheld your son, your favored one, I will bestow My blessing on you and make your descendants as numerous as the stars in heaven" (Gen. 22:16–17).

The Midrash expresses surprise that the divine blessing depends explicitly on this test (this specific test: "because you have done *this*"), which is already the tenth one! "One must understand that the injunction to sacrifice represents the last of the tests [whence its qualification by *zeh*], and is in itself the equivalent of all the others in one; if he had not agreed to submit to it, Abraham would have lost *everything*" (*Midrash Rabbah*, Gen. 56:11). Here we see, in an entirely classical manner, an extrapolation of the demonstrative as an expression of proximity. This test, the most immediate in time, is thus chronologically the last. This chronology is hierarchized into a system of values: the last, and therefore the hardest, as every heroic story assumes—even a moral one. However, one cannot understand this midrash in depth unless one restores the coded value to the words: *zeh*, "this," and *kol*, "all," participate in the same reality: "And because 'all' depends on this Sphere (*Yesod*), the latter is rendered by the word 'all' (*Sha'aré Orah*, p. 57). The last test set for Abraham, designated by *zeh*, is of the order of that virtue called *kol*, which simultaneously establishes, on the psychological and moral level, the test's decisive character.

Here is a final example of this hermeneutic ambivalence that, beneath the almost redundant explanation of a deictic functioning, conceals a precise semantic intention: "The Lord freed us from Egypt . . . and brought us to this place" (Deut. 26:8–9). "And brought us to this place: this refers to the Temple" (*Sifré*, Deut. 319 L 11). The commentary seems to want to circumscribe the context of utterance: speaking *in the Temple*, the bearer of the first fruits thus designates precisely his immediate surroundings. However, the midrash uses this punctual and ephemeral deictic situation to broaden it to the particulars of a "full" sign. Here *zeh* determines its reference, not in a mechanical way, but because it is linked with it in other ways, for example, conventionally (through the semantic transitivity of *Yesod* [*zeh*] and of *Malkhuth* [Temple]).

The midrashim centered on *zot* develop the themes of *Mal-*

khuth into a single, still allusive coherence: "By this (*zot*), you shall know that I am the Lord" (Exod. 7:17): "When a man wants to bring some misfortune on his enemy, he acts in a sudden fashion, keeping his enemy from seeing it. The Holy One, blessed-be-He, on the contrary, *warns* Pharaoh before each of the plagues, in order to lead him to repent. Thus one finds it written: 'By this (*zot*) you shall know that I am the Lord'" (*Midrash Rabbah*, Exod. 9:9). The notion of warning is drawn from an immediate future linked to the presence of the demonstrative. Behind this inference, the semanticization of *zot* responds to a precise thematics—here, the virtue of *Judgment* unveiled in the modality of *Malkhuth*, which metes out retribution and punishes. This character of judgment reappears in a second midrash, within the same general context (Pharaoh's obstinacy) but concerning a different verse: "And Pharaoh turned and went into his palace, paying no regard even to this (*zot*)" (Exod. 7:23). "He did not fear the plague with which divine justice struck him, and was not moved by it" (*Midrash Rabbah*, Exod. 9:11).

REFERENTIAL EQUIVALENCE

We will also take up, alongside these ambiguities in the workings of sense, the case of equations founded on discourse. One finds the same gap between apparent technique and the actual semanticization, which here again leads to a conventional model.

"This very month (*zeh*) shall be for you the first of the months [marking the departure from Egypt]" (Exod. 12:2). One of the numerous commentaries on this verse is content to add laconically: "This expression refers us to the text of the Song of Solomon: 'it is the voice of my beloved! That (*zeh*) is he coming' (Song of Sol. 2:8)" (*Chemot Rabba*, Exod. 15:1). The sense of this comparison is explained by the idea of deliverance. The *saving* God, He "who comes," already revealed Himself in the modality of *zeh*[20] at the time of the *departure from Egypt*, in "the first of the months." The parallelism imposed by the midrash, and repeated in the ritual (which provides for reading the Song of Solomon in the month of the deliverance from Egypt), goes beyond a purely chance recurrence.

Another example, concerning the Levites descended from the family of Kehath: "Do this (*zot*) with them, that they may live and not die when they approach the most sacred objects . . . " (Num. 4:19): "Do this: just as one finds written concerning Aaron (Lev. 16:3): This (*zot*) is how Aaron shall enter the Shrine, so here it is the word *zot* that is used. . . . A repetition that lets us understand that these four families—Gershon, Kehath, Merari, Aaron and his sons—surround the *meeting tent* in order to receive *Providence* there" (*Midrash Rabbah*, Num. 6:7–8). This equivalence becomes legible only through the connotations it evokes (or reconstructs) within the thematic framework of *Malkhuth*, and which include, in this precise case, the signifieds "meeting tent" and "Providence."

These first cases were still regulated by the classical forms of exegesis, set forth above in chapters 1 and 2, whose premises they transcended in the direction of an autonomous thematization. In a second stage, the semanticization of *zeh* becomes less and less justifiable by the immediate features of the text.[21]

In one case the midrash elides the preliminary forms of the reasoning, as in the following model, where *zeh* is related, through a truncated *gezerah shavah*,[22] to the Holy One: "And he [Joseph] replied: 'I am looking for my brothers; could you tell me where they are pasturing?' The man said, 'They have gone from *here* (*mizeh*)'" (Gen. 37:16–17). Here is the midrash's commentary (*Midrash Rabbah*, Gen. 84:4): "They have gone away from *here* (= from *zeh*): they turned away from the virtues of the '*place*.'"[23]

This explication is developed by the *Midrash Rabbah* commentator,[24] who restores the implicit textual equivalence: "They have strayed from the virtues of the Holy One, blessed-be-He, *who is called zeh*, in accordance with the verse 'This (*zeh*) is my God' (Exod. 15:2): goodness, grace and mercy count among

His virtues." The clarification contributed by this (later) commentator is very illuminating, in that it underscores the laconic character of the Midrashic formulation.

Such a punctual interpretation, which presents itself as an independent parabolic teaching, ultimately leads, by way of a concealed textual equation, to the thematic class of *Yesod*, into which "God," "place" (through *Tifereth* [Rabbi M. Codovero]), and even "Joseph" are integrated.

In the other case, the exegesis asserts itself in the present, in the lesson of each reading, outside any hermeneutic continuity. The principle of a thematic determination still remains valid and projects its grids onto the calculated dispersion of the commentary: "When Lamech had lived 182 years, he begot a son. And he named him Noah ["the reliever"], saying 'This one (*zeh*) will provide us relief from our work and from the toil of our hands, out of the very soil which the Lord placed under a curse'" (Gen. 5:28–29): "'This one (*zeh*) will provide us relief': A just man comes into the world, he brings calm (*tova*) with him. That is what we are told by the verse: 'This one (*zeh*) will provide us relief from our work and from the toil of our hands'" (*Sanhedrin* 113b).

The identification of *zeh* as Tzaddik, the "just man," is not surprising; in this particular context, the immediate reference of the demonstrative is the figure of Noah, "a just man in his generation," as the Bible says. The correlation established with the equilibrium of the world, while it lays down the important theme of an interdependence of the moral life and the natural life, is nonetheless also perfectly consistent with the immediate context. However, beyond that truth, a precise network of significations surfaces for anyone who can read the necessary allusion beneath the contingent exposition, which is instructive in itself: "*zeh*," the "just man" and the "good" (*tovah*), as specific themes, belong to the same family of expression and spiritual experience: that of the *Sephirah* of *Yesod*.[25]

This relation between *zeh* and the Tzaddik is repeated by another midrash, but in a more indirect manner, to the extent to which the (direct) reference of the demonstrative is not mentioned in it: "This (*zeh*) is none other than the abode of God,

and this (*zeh*) is the gateway to heaven" (Gen. 28:17): "Rabbi
Aha teaches us: this (*zeh*) gateway is called to open one day to
many *just men* like you" (*Midrash Rabbah*, Gen. 69:7). On first
reading, the parable is only moralizing; it illuminates the conduct of the Fathers with a promise of a future. Behind it, a
whole sphere of achievement is intended.[26]

This last example leads us toward cases where the commentary's grammatical point of articulation is more in doubt.
They present themselves as independent motifs and exceed the
limits of a regular (i.e., structurally defined) semanticization.[27]
Incapable of founding the analysis by themselves, they still
confirm it for anyone who acknowledges—within the multitude of themes proposed, and for which only a computer could
calculate the proportions—the insistent recurrence of certain
sequences.

EXTENSIONS

We will enter into this symbolic play with the precautions
proper for conjecture and intuition: how far should we push
the implicit semantic coherence, when it is no longer frozen in
the ice of a clear textual logic?

"And Moses said to the people, Remember this (*zeh*) day, on
which you went free from Egypt, the house of bondage" (Exod.
13:3): "And warn the children of Israel: just as I have created
the world and enjoined you to remember the *Sabbath*, which
commemorates the creation [since it is written: 'Remember the
sabbath day' (Exod. 20:8)], in the same way remember the miracles that I performed for you in Egypt and the day you went
out of it, as it is said in the verse: 'Remember *this* (*zeh*) day, on
which you went free from Egypt'" (*Midrash Rabbah*, Exod. 19:7).

The analogy between the creation of the world and the departure from Egypt as a double historicity is a fundamental
given of the Jewish tradition; onto it is grafted a second level
of coherence. "*Remember this* day": what the midrash adds, under the redundancy of the designation, is the allusion to another commemoration, that of the *Sabbath*, the unveiling in cos-

mic time (like the *departure from Egypt* in history) of the sphere of *Yesod*, and connoted by *zeh*.[28]

In the same book of the *Midrash Rabbah* on Exodus, a little further on, we encounter, apropos of a verse in Deuteronomy, the extension of *zot* by "sea," conventionally founded on the *Sephirah* of *Malkhuth*: "Is this (*zot*) how you requite the Lord?" (Deut. 32:6). "This" is explained by the midrash in the following manner: "You rebelled on the Red *Sea* after so many miracles!" (*Midrash Rabbah*, Exod. 24:1).[29]

If we acknowledge a semantic transfer between the spheres (a transitivity postulated by the exegesis itself),[30] in the following commentary we can isolate the association of *zeh* with "blessing": "Jacob said to his father, 'I am Esau, your first-born; I have done as you told me. Pray sit up and eat of my game, that you may give me your innermost blessing.' Isaac said to his son, 'What is *this* (*zeh*)? You have succeeded so quickly, my son!'" (Gen. 27: 19–20). Now here, according to the midrash, is what causes Isaac's astonishment ("What is this?"): "You have succeeded so quickly in finding the *blessing*, my son; your father was blessed only at the age of 75, and you already at 63" (*Midrash Rabbah*, Gen. 65:19).

In order to support this demonstration, let us test the insertion of the partial thematics developed here in the matrices.

For *zeh*:

- "They have gone away from *here*" .... the virtues of the Holy-blessed-be-He (Gen. 37:17)
- "*This* very month shall be for you" .... the lover (God) (Exod. 12:2)
- "*This* must be a Hebrew child" .... circumcision (Exod. 2:6)
- "*This* one will provide us relief" .... the just man (Tzaddik) (Gen. 5:29)
- "*This* is none other than God's abode" .... the just man (Tzaddik) (Gen. 28:17)
- "Because you have done *this*" .... all (Gen. 22:16)

} *zeh*

- "And he led us to *this* place" .... Temple (Deut. 26:9)
- "Remember *this* day" (Exod. 13:3) .... Sabbath

} Mixed table

For *zot*:

- "By *this* you shall know" (Exod. 7:17) ..... severity, judgment ⎫
- "Is *this* how you requite" (Deut. 32:6) ..... sea   ⎬ *zot*
- And *this* is what you shall do" .... Meeting tent,   ⎭
  (Num. 4:19)   Providence

And an example of transition:

- "What is *this*? You have been . . . . blessing ⎫ *zot*
  prompt to find" (Gen. 27:20)   ⎭

For the coincidence of terms, see the tables in chapter 3.[31]

Thus there are many examples that testify to a general circumscription and encoding of Midrash by the symbolic structures of Sod.

INTERPRETATION OF THE RESULTS

We have not concealed the leading idea of this location of themes: to discern in them a complex of parallel symbols, associated by exegesis with the occurrence of the demonstrative, at each level of interpretation. This more or less marked general convergence of all hermeneutic registers toward that of Sod leads the investigator to acknowledge the anagogic axes as *determining* with respect to the first levels of signification, and to recognize in them the connoted planes (S2 and R2) that governed the exegesis's selection of both constitutive sememes (S2) and privileged references (R2). We can deduce therefrom the invisible but powerful structuration "in depth" of Midrashic commentary, on a conventional basis of kabbalistic orientation,[32] which opens a breach in the barriers separating the levels of interpretation.

We can also better understand the notion, repeated several times, of the *inversion of determination* (see chaps. 1 and 2). The latter must be extended to all dimensions of exegesis, whose progression must be turned upside down. Hermeneutics does not arbitrarily deepen its furrows from a simple reading to a more essential decoding. The stress on a progressive integration of the elementary facts of interpretation in the thematic network of Sod makes it possible to reestablish their subterranean hierarchy, tracked thus far in reversals of detail. We will in fact postulate, on the basis of these repeated coincidences, from Peshat to Sod, the *semantic preeminence* of anagogic identification, which is like a horizon line toward which all the perspectives of the first levels of exegesis point. This new literality represented by Sod, which is the first true sense of the text and the word, is deferred until the fourth stage of interpretation as a final acknowledgment, but it conditions and leaves its mark on the preliminary stages. A "deep structure,"[33] and thus secret, the truth of sense generates partial senses and truths touched upon, which manifest it, in one or another moment of the reading. If the strata of interpretation are not mutually exclusive, if they do not disappear as sense progresses toward sense, if they are not only compatible but simultaneously true, concomitant, that is because they all proceed, in varying degrees of unveiling and at autonomous levels of inquiry, from a single code, which is hidden but precise and ramified into its semantic correspondences.[34]

The questions raised by these comparisons, and in general by the coherence brought out, are numerous. This coherence draws attention first of all to the principle of a hermeneutic *truth*, of a coded transcendence of signification, the ultimate reference on which all senses would founder.[35] The risk of stifling exegetical inspiration seems to be immediate.

The thematic convergence brought out does not, however, disconfirm the autonomy of each procedure, or the coherence of fragmentary solutions within a given system. This recomposition of underlying grids results from an a posteriori development. The independence of the levels of signification is safeguarded both by the homogeneity, the specificity, of each hermeneutic procedure and by a notorious begging of the question that prohibits dismantling one level of interpretation to the advantage of the next.[36] In spite of the overlaps from one register to another, the methods of Peshat, Derash, and Remez are peculiar to them in every case and are not reined in by any thematic limit.

In particular, we must recognize that the parabolic level has maximum autonomy with respect to the conditioning of Sod.

If a hierarchy looms, and makes us read semantic networks under the punctual explication, its mark is not absolute, nor is its application systematic. Midrash, as we have seen, corresponds to a degree of actualization that draws the multiplicity of its projections from the existential. As such, it is not subject in an overall fashion to the expectations of the mystical structuration.

The convergence is recognized but never imposed. Each register calls forth, according to its own laws of reading, new combinations, none of which can be invalidated or rejected by the superior register in the name of its very superiority. The strata are superimposed and guarantee each other reciprocally, without ever erasing each other or substituting themselves for one another. The most sophisticated anagogic interpretation cannot "surmount" the immediate reading.

This openness of the process, which is fundamental from the point of view of the rabbinical sensibility, seems to be guaranteed in traditional exegesis by the essentially polysemous nature of sense and by the indeterminacy of its system of combination. We recall in this regard the mobility of the series brought out by Sod and the doubled organization of its codes. Anagogic interpretation presents itself in fact as a double-registered structure, as a perception that is multiplied at the same time that it is univocal.

The uncertainty of the retranslations is inscribed in this gap that places at the keystone of each *Sephirah*, as the very place of its (global) signification, an empty structure, a mathematical, abstract line, open to the dissemination of references. The correspondence cannot therefore operate minutely, from term to term: rather, it embraces complex classes, constructs motives. Its function is integrative, a relation inscribed in a semantic field that is extensible in its turn—and perhaps modified by this very inscription.

This uncertainty is itself significant, since these boundary stones of anagogy, placed at the four corners of interpretation, would limit its burgeoning energy if convention could determine or constrain, rather than inspire, the reading. The posited tension between exactitude and disorder is central to our subject, and far from being diminished by these preliminary remarks, it will become increasingly intense and acute as the analysis proceeds. However, this juxtaposition of the results, showing a synchronic coherence of the levels of interpretation, and calling for the hypothesis that they are conditioned by Sod, contravenes the expectations of a historicist criticism that posits an evolution of commentary (an arbitrary and discontinuous evolution) but agrees with the belief in the transtemporal unity of rabbinical exegesis.[37]

One could cite, to support the historical thesis, a systematic coding of Midrashic narratives, achieved by the kabbalists a posteriori from parabolic exegesis, and basing its paradigms on contextual associations *already* pointed out by Midrash. But then we would not be able to get out of the vicious circle that draws these conventional grids from Midrash and then measures them by its standard.

However, this theory does not cover the whole of the phenomena pointed out, once one has gone beyond the mere semantic juxtaposition of units to study the modes of derivation that connect them. The superimposition of distinct logics is hard to reconcile with the idea of a later reconstruction of the codes. It leads us on the contrary to seek a broader principle of integration, within which the thematic coincidence would be only a particular effect. In this reversal of priorities, Midrash illustrates but does not found sense, except to the extent to which the diverse lines of interpretation, for reasons of functional equivalence that will be taken up later, become concurrent.

This synchrony of readings, unveiled along with the junction of the semantic series, thus requires us to rethink the functioning of signification. The thematic convergence, the result of empirical juxtapositions, supposes a transitivity of the structures and a retranslation allowed by the codes. It is this retranscription, the rules that govern its application and its categories, that we must now examine, insofar as they manifest, behind the laws of the constitution and transposition of sense, a philosophy of language. It is in the mechanism of these equations, which superimpose specific speech acts on a linguistic system, a textual reference on a conventional signification, a systematic elaboration on an analogical derivation of sense—it is in the conditions of the validity of these recognitions and these translations that the true key of exegesis is coiled up, in its methods and its contents.

Beyond the thematic convergence, even beyond the laws of its functioning, it is clearly the very possibility of a convergence, and the existence of these laws, that produces and, drawing on the whole of the hermeneutic experience, translates both the idea of Truth and the idea of its representation in the text.

5

Transitivities

The first chapters of this work presented two main axes of reference for the reading of the demonstrative pronoun, one contextual,[1] the other conventional. One, based on the deictic character of *zeh*, began from the grammatical category to reinsert it into the discourse; the other drew up the table of *zeh*'s semantic values in a mystical coded language. Two parallel (and inverse) paths run side by side here. On one hand, on the basis of the structures of the text, a subtle semantic construction develops a series of connoted actualizations. On the other, a network of symbols projects an organized thematic ensemble into each term of the sacred language. "Textual" hermeneutics proper, which brings together the first three levels of exegesis (Peshat, Remez, and Derash), is thus radically distinguished, by its semantic relations as well as by the laws of its functioning, from the solutions governed by anagogy.

This rather summary presentation—which in particular reduces the kabbalistic vision to a static system of correlations—nevertheless underscores the fundamental opposition between these two semiotic approaches, an opposition that gravitates around the principle of motivation. It is well known that contemporary reflection on language distinguishes these two perspectives and considers them incompatible. In the textual-linguistic dimension, the element is defined, classically, "at the same time as its place" (here, in writing); whereas anagogic interpretation offers a fixed translation of the sign, in a biunivocal and motivated relation that escapes the constraints of its use "in situation."

This confrontation of the sign (on the text side) and the symbol (on the code side) makes the convergence described in the preceding chapter all the more astonishing. In particular, it allows us to glimpse, behind this double exegetical route, the integration of the textual level of signification into the symbolic network of hidden representations—since the different methods of reading do not appear to be concurrent, but on the contrary intersect the same results.

This is a theoretical proposition of convergence that calls, on the plane of method, for a revision of the categories of sense and of the forms of its determination. Its paradoxical character, as the principle of the reconciliation of contraries, will be maintained on the ideological plane. On the logical plane, it can be reformulated, if not reduced, by a redistribution of the problem's givens. One can propose basing the concurrence of hermeneutic decisions on intermediate forms of the structuration of sense that have ambivalent criteria. They are discovered at all levels of exegesis, preparing transitions yet to come.

But it is above all the Kabbalah that transcends and rejects divisions foreign to its spirit. Its complex formation presents a system of combination sufficiently subtle to integrate into its reading orders of signification that appear to be heterogenous. In the Kabbalah original mechanisms are defined that include several types of code—in which one can recognize, conjointly, a *semiotic* system and a *symbolic* system of interpretation.

CATEGORIAL TRANSITIVITY

At a first stage of analysis the linguistic code and the (mystical) symbolic are juxtaposed in an overall semiological perspective. In this relationship between languages—the language of Peshat and that of Sod—we shall study the planes of signification as such, the definition of the levels of sense (linguistic or metalinguistic), and not the particular thematic references they derive.[2]

The Connoted Circuit

From Peshat to Remez, Jewish hermeneutics treats biblical Hebrew as an "unmotivated" natural language, in the contemporary sense of the arbitrariness of the sign.[3] The working of language, before the text and then in it, does not fail to recall the complex paragrams of any sophisticated literary exercise with its multiple resonances.

In this type of total text in which all senses are at play, we will take a general law of *connotation* to be the organizing principle. On the basis of a simple term this law of connotation recomposes the layers of interpretation that enclose each other. It causes a movement from a primary grammatical sense, that of designation (S1), to the connoted sense (S2) of "revelation" (corresponding to the coded "sense" of the demonstrative) through the intermediate stages of thematization or contextualization. This schema in the manner of Roland Barthes can explain the table of homologous planes of signification presented in the preceding chapter.

The "demonstrative" sememe selected by the Peshat as the pertinent sense of *zeh* allows us to note within the utterance a series of immediate references in accord with the classical laws of *deixis*. This demonstrative sense defined in the linguistic system *connotes* at the same time a trait of uniqueness and specificity that in discourse takes on a value of "concretization" or "proximity," which is recognized as "thematic." Without challenging the immediate references posited by a first-degree understanding, this allows exegesis to double the reading of these references by referential connotations of a parabolic type. This general trait of "cognition" or "recognition," which includes the partial thematizations of demonstrative sense, connotes in turn the figurative trait of "revelation" or "presence" that runs through all the contexts in which *zeh* appears.

Moreover, the notation of the references selected by Midrash in the juxtaposition of contexts leads, we recall, to a coherent semantic ensemble. To that extent, the overall signified attached to this recomposition could be seen as *connoted* with respect to the partial sense unveiled in each fragmentary referentialization and as anticipating in other respects the thematic lines of the Sod.

From level to level, the process of connotation, whether it focuses directly on the demonstrative sense or passes through the contextual (or projective, in the sense of a projection onto the real through the reader's subjectivity) detour of its references, always ends up rejoining this signified belonging to a superior level and inspiring each sememe.

Hence the table of "thematic convergence" given in chapter 4 (p. 103) appears coherent: the sense takes on new traits at each intersection, in accord with the resources of the language, the rhetoric of the reading, and the richness of the cultural codes.

THE SYMBOLIC CIRCUIT

However, a parallel axis of senses was unveiled along with the analysis of the anagogic system. Endowed with autonomous coordinates, this plane of interpretation in fact presented itself— at least a priori—as radically independent, completely cut off from the lower levels. The specific sense attached to the demonstrative no longer passed by way of its comprehension in context. Its "absolute" deciphering was no longer subject to the chances of linguistic play but was grasped directly, in an inalienable fashion, in a new language that was that of the Sod.

This indifference to the contextual environment of the sign, and in particular to the evocatory effects of connotation, comes out clearly in the schema in chapter 3 (p. 96), where through the strata of signification one can recognize a correspondence, immediate but with multiple modalities, between a term in the language and the anagogic sense associated with it. The whole is codified in accord with the tropes of any kabbalistic lexicon one chooses.[4] In this apparently static arrangement, the sense is reproduced without being modified. The language at work in the generation of the text is here determined in analogical relays. The *semiotic* relation between levels becomes *symbolic*.[5]

Parallel to the order of *connotations*, a sequence of successive *representations* allows us to arrive as well, on the basis of an initial logogram—in our case, the term *zeh*—at the mystical idea of holiness, the presence of the sacred within the world. These analogical sequences are based on the configuration of the word itself, before its entry into the arena of discourse, and in its double reality as a sign: as signifier and as signified.[6]

To push the paradox further and to underscore the deep disparity of the functionings, we shall first take up this symbolic observation from the point of view of the signifier, which stresses its emblematic character. At the same time we leave the strictly linguistic universe and its rules, in order to find ideographic forms of sense notation in a rather complex system that participates simultaneously in pictographic writing and alphabetic phoneticization. Whatever its precise symbolic value, this writing links signs and mental images, or signs and other signs, without necessarily passing by way of verbal signification proper. As in any relationship of symbolization, this association is motivated, and based on conceptual homologies (on the ideographic side) or formal homologies (on the alphabetic notation side).

Insofar as it is a form, the linguistic signifier refers to other forms that echo it but do not exhaust its symbolic capacity: it *signifies* just as much by the very arrangement of its letters as by the acrostic or numerical value linked with them, or by the (monematic) radical that they constitute. Halfway between the abstract modern phonetic writing of Western languages (where "the graphic sign denotes a nonmeaningful linguistic unit")[7] and the directly representative pictographic writing of more ancient cultures, the Hebraic sign thus secretes, by its very configuration, a sort of "signified-of-the-signifier" distinct from the linguistic signified proper through which the word is included in language;[8] this "formal signified" engenders in turn numerical, lexical, or literal series that can be figuratively associated with it (see the table in chap. 3, p. 96).

Thus *zeh*, by the form of the letter ה, which is part of its makeup, assumes a feminine principle (connected with *Malkhuth*). The curve of the ה in fact turns backward to represent the concavity of the receptacle, the matricial/uterine reservoir of all fecundity. Concurrently, by its numerical value, it "signifies" twelve, the conventional number of totality, related to the *Sephirah* of *Yesod*.[9]

But these two figurative modes are themselves in an osmotic relationship: the "signifier" circuit and the "signified" circuit alternate so as to extend the sequence of representations. Through the common denominator of a semantic *or* formal analogy, substitutions of signs are permitted, and themselves enter into play as new symbolic reflections: if *zeh* indicates "twelve" by the sum of its letters, then other signs, which through the same process of addition arrive at the same number, are thus possible substitutes for it—forming along with *zeh* an analogical paradigm (see the schema below).

In the same way, *vav*, the name of the sixth letter of the Hebrew alphabet, which is formed by doubling the letter *vav* (with a value of 6), has a total value of twelve. But once again *vav*, which is both the letter and the name of the letter, is multiplied in complementary strata of expression. By its numerical value (and by its place in the alphabet), it belongs to a base-6 calculus, as well as to the associated analogical series. By its graphical form, ו, it also represents a vertical mark that represents in turn other straight marks and other verticalities. The straight line itself is both a form and a signification, both an image and a structure, and develops its own symbolic recurrences.[10]

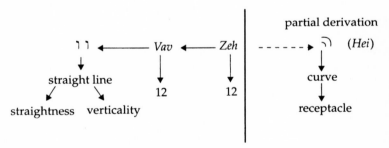

What is remarkable here, from the point of view of biblical semiotics, is that the scale of representations crosses the strata of connoted senses within one another. The two movements, which pertain to two heterogeneous orders of the sign (in the general sense of the term) and to two universes of language, lead to the same results. From number to letter, from figure to idea, the Hebrew word discovers in the diffraction of its symbols the ultimate sense called for by the *text*: through the image of the straight line or through the signification of unveiling, the semantics of *zeh* always arrives at the *revelation of a Presence.*

Underlying that compatibility is the equivalence of the sign and the symbol that is *proposed*, in a language that is poetic through-and-through, but with the exactness of a metaphysician's poetry.

Synthesis: Metaphorization

To follow these mechanisms of equivalence, we have to take the antagonisms between systems at their point of tangency. The symbolic organization of the Kabbalah is not monolithic, in that it is secondarily based on effects that are properly linguistic. The initial sign, to which the sequence of successive representations is connected, is in fact pictographic only to a certain degree. In the mystical figuration, the word *also* retains the value of signification *that comes to it from the language,* and which in turn makes possible translation operations of an uncertain nature, which will be covered by the general term *metaphorization.* The latter repeats the echo of a single signified at different levels of perception, and in a relationship of analogy; it is then *very close* to textual functioning, and in particular to the effects of thematization recognized as *connoted*: the latter appear in turn linked by a symbolic and motivated relation that merges the itineraries.

We recall that the linguistic indications attached to the demonstrative sense, as pure linguistic instructions in the location of a reference, were semanticized by taking on the value of a thematic determination and defined the specificity of the designated object. This essentialization of the grammatical givens, which infers a qualification on the basis of the use values of a term, is here extended to the various levels of interpretation. We can thus recognize, in the "absolute" comprehension that would make *zeh* the "proper" designation of the Divinity, a "hypostasis" of its demonstrative function.

If in fact we go back to the characteristic traits of demonstrative sense, we can easily track down the elements favoring
a generalized metaphorization:

a) Limited to the demonstrative function, *deixis* does not fail
to posit a deep relationship between its general process of actualization and the *presupposition of existence*. Thus to speak of
the object is already to assume its reality: "In so far as the very
fact of pointing to something commits the person who is pointing to a belief in the existence of what he is pointing at, the
use of a deictic pronoun carries with it the implication or presupposition of existence. The act of reference does this any-
way: but there is perhaps some reason to believe that there is
a deeper connexion between deixis and the presupposition of
existence."[11]

b) The perception of existence is at first linked to the concrete environment, to the *proximate presence* of the object to the
speaking subject: "The expressions designating existence go
back to spatial notions."[12]

But the linguist already foresees an extension of this immediate knowledge and a displacement of the sememe of designation; there remains an experience that is transposable to
absent realities but marking the utterance with their imprint:
"What is essential to the hypothesis is merely the assumption
that the function of demonstrative pronouns in languages is
first learned in actual situations-of-utterance with reference to
entities present in the situational context. Taking this to be their
basic and ontogenetically prior function, we can see how they
might later come to be used with reference to entities removed
in space and time from the situation-of-utterance."[13]

c) Finally, this *relation to the other* seems to fulfill the demonstrative function and to exhaust it entirely in a pure designation: testifying to a presence, the demonstrative "merely designates an object without in any degree describing it";[14] it does
not grasp the essence, or diagnose any content, but only expresses the speaker's experience of an encounter.

By itself, the formulation of these pertinent traits already
suggests the goal they project, beyond a first-degree psycho-
linguistic system, onto the upper register of the values of truth,

in the ethical and logical sense. The presupposition of existence, the experience of proximity in distance, an unplumbable exteriority—these characteristics that are at first mere linguistic supports are radicalized and appear definitional. They are "substantialized" and become a quality in itself of the thing designated. Ultimately, they even suffice, without the appearance of an object-term, to connote presence. This final link in the chain founds the anagogic reading, which finds in *zeh* an indirect evocation of the divine. God is indeed the awakener par excellence, the Ungraspable and the Recognized. Thus all experience of the relationship refers in the end to Being in itself, as it is perceived by Jewish sensibility, simultaneously nearby and distant, as an attentive permanence. An indirect presence of Providence, in every case of the use of the demonstrative, designates the Omnipresence behind the screen of each designation.[15]

This is a necessary semantic displacement that has ambiguous modalities: a posteriori on the basis of these analyses we can recognize in this metaphorization the completed merger of semantic connotation and analogical symbolization. An indication of its structural ambivalence is provided by the uncertainty of the (axial) direction of the derivation: the *connotation* seems to go toward a psychology of the hidden and, on the basis of an initial demonstrative sense, to lead to the intuition of a transcendence.

But the process is inverted in the prophetic range of the Bible: for Hebraic consciousness, it is from the original trauma of absolute Presence that is deduced the perception of all presence. The relationship between these experiences is thus clearly *symbolic* and manifests, in each reality, a possible revelation, a diluted sign of the Revelation. The demonstrative is thus called on for the linguistic exercise of designation, in a metaphorical grammatical usage of its initial use, which is to recognize the Unknowable, to explode proximity, but at first outside any grasp or definition. Conjointly with the semantic mechanism of the "hypostasis" of the demonstrative sense, a correspondence of a mimetic order is thus realized: as if the act of ostension of an immediate environment were *ritualized* in order to recognize the absolute. These marginal phenomena, which represent no more than an aspect of the organizing law internal to each ensemble, at least make it possible for these ensembles to come together in limit-cases.

Thematization, the first anomaly in the syntagmatic relationship of the determinant to the determined object, is nevertheless integrated into the textual system of connotations, which includes other forms of determination and displacement of sense (for example, the restructuring of references). Moreover, qua metaphorization, this thematization can also be integrated into a scale of representations as the allegorical reflection of superior realities; and this can be done concurrently with other types of symbolic transposition produced not on the basis of signifieds but through forms or numbers.

Thematization thus focuses within itself and illustrates the possibility of a coincidence of the *order of sense* and the *order of representation*. It manifests at its own level the principle, marked differently in each case, of an essential transition between the *semiological* and the *represented* in biblical language.[16]

FUNCTIONAL TRANSITIVITY

These conclusions can be carried over into the analysis of the *references* noted at each level of interpretation. Tracked on parallel planes of signification, and in a relationship of connotation or symbolization, the coincidence of the referential units located is explained by a general metaphorization that translates each sign into a superior register of encoding. Thus "woman," "water," or "Temple" is repeated from one level to another, translated by allegory.

Even when deferred, the coincidence of parabolic and contextual references poses a new problem, which symbolic or connotative structuring does not suffice to resolve. We recall in fact that the thematic derivations of the demonstrative on the coded level were defined as *referential* by analogy with the mechanisms of *actualization* of *deixis* in discourse. However, these semantic determinations proceed from very different techniques, which do not normally arrive at congruent results. If the ref-

erences noted in discourse are deduced from a textual configuration (*Remez*), the "references" defined by Sod (the anagogic
level) are derived *systematically* on the basis of an initial semantic nucleus—on one hand, the plasticity of living speech; on the
other, the rigidity of complexes already constituted by the dictionaries.[17]

To this two-term convergence between the text and the
outside-the-text is added yet another protean element, specific
to *Derash*, which is its existential coefficient, that is, the whole
of the possible exponents, with differing indices of reality, of
a demonstrative sense reread by the subjectivity of the commentator.[18]

What the convergence of signs reveals, even in the details
of their derivation, is here again, and perhaps more surpris-
ingly, the *compatibility of the text and the code*, but as a folding
back of the speech act onto the linguistic system, of the aleatory onto the predictable. Here again, as in the analysis of the
planes of signification, or of overall semiotic systems, we shall
bring out the intermediate structures, a new way of reading
sense that escapes classification and presents itself by its very
nature as ambivalent. Once again it is the Kabbalah that provides the elements of this synthesis, integrating the lower levels of interpretation, even on the functional plane. All the modes
of signifying and their system of combinations can be seen as
particular cases of an overall system that associates mobile (textual) traits and coded traits.

Under its secret influence, the law of interpretation at each
level is opened to *mixed* examples, whose duality we shall examine, in particular, in the processes of *contextualization*, the relationship between actual syntagms and the systematics of references. For Jewish exegesis, in spite of its strata, it is in fact
the text that represents the supreme authority. The fact that
it appears alternately as origin or as projection of sense—depending on whether the referential derivation is drawn from
a syntactic logic or imposed on it in rigid series—presupposes
the indeterminacy of the functionings that govern it.

This combination of the complementary parameters of the
linguistic system and of the speech act defines a hybrid mode

of expression, recognized as a *metalanguage*, which can serve as the keystone of a system of interpretation that posits this synthesis as its very principle.

The Relation of Signification

At the level of Remez, the play of contexts in biblical discourse sketches out a broad network of syntagmatic relations, and in this way, starting from the distribution of *zeh* it arranges a referential field of the demonstrative, whose contours we sketched in chapter 2. However, it already appeared at that level of the study that its structuration, as its stages were passed through by exegesis, had differing degrees of syntactical coherence.

a) *Direct* referentialization, defined as a semantic link between the demonstrative and its "determinant," covers the majority of the cases of *zeh*'s occurrence. We find this classical usage in utterances of the type: "This is the land that shall fall to you as your portion" (Num. 34:2), where *zot* (this) is semanticized into "land" (*Sha'aré Orah*, p. 28), or "This is the law" (Num. 19:2), which "actualizes" *zot* as *Hukah*, the law, on the basis of agreement in gender (*Sha'aré Orah*, p. 53).

b) The referential relationship can be less evident, that is, based on a *general* context of signification, without direct grammatical relation between determinant and determined object.

Exegesis, as we have seen, thus takes some license with pure linguistic analysis, and broadens the principle to an ensemble of contextual themes. The complex expression "vezot Liyehudah," for example, "And this he said of Judah" (literally, And this, *to* Judah) (Deut. 33:7), is repeated in the midrash as an immediate determination, without the interpreter being halted by the indirect form of the complement "of signification." This greater tolerance in the effects of semanticization opens the way to larger and larger complexes that would quickly approach a grammar of signifieds of a structuralist type.

Most often, this thematic extension is based on an attributive function, in which exegesis recognizes (and systematizes) a semantic equivalence. When, for example, Moses' mother gives birth to her son, the child's deep nature is already revealed:

"And she saw that he was good" (Exod. 2:2). A qualification that allows the *Sha'aré Orah* to link "good" with "Moses," and by transitivity—through "Moses"—to the demonstrative *"zeh"* attached to him (this time in a relationship of direct referentialization): "This man Moses" (Exod. 32:1).[19]

Thus are constituted grids that are more or less clearly based on the formulation of the verses. The Kabbalah takes them up and radicalizes them in its textual commentaries.

We recall, in fact, that Midrash under mystical influence[20] resolved these thematic associations in the direction of a univocal and autonomized relation.[21] Thus in the following example, where Gemara seeks only to make a referential context explicit, and interprets as "Messiah" the one of whom "this (*zeh*) is the name": "The-Lord-is-my-righteousness" (Jer. 23:6). The Kabbalah systematizes the (grammatically indirect) determination: *zeh*, as such, *signifies* henceforth "the Messiah" (*Bava Bathra* 75b; taken up by the kabbalists: *Ir Giborim, Bo,* and *Sefer Erké Hakinuyim,* entries *zeh* and *Mashiah*).

The recurrent references noted by Midrash are declared to be characteristic and are codified by anagogic interpretation. This risk taken by exegesis, apropos of less evident contexts, to the point of advancing clear implications, cannot be understood as grammatical carelessness. In a world of interpretation so permeated by linguistic sensibility, these assemblages of signifieds respect semantic rules acknowledged by the language, but no doubt based on conventions that remain external to them: at the boundaries of its usage, contextual determination rigidifies into a systematic determination.

The Relation of Juxtaposition

At the other extreme, we find an opposite mode of tracking references: the one proposed by mysticism, a priori, in advance of the contextualization of the demonstrative. Chapter 3 presented, on a conventional basis, a table of these possible semantics. But here again, the definitions must be reformulated.

If contextuality stumbles, in an uncertain moment of its recomposition, toward a surer hidden ordering, the paradigmatic

series of Sod also return to draw from the biblical text the reflection of their configuration.

Kabbalistic exposition includes in its argument, as we have
seen, broad extracts from biblical discourse that have an ambiguous status. In the course of the demonstration, these quotations are mixed with the anagogic gridding and challenge its
foundations. Whatever its argumentative value might be, the
appeal to the text makes the mystical teaching stumble from a
purely logical or conventional thematics toward a complementary *linguistic* basis—of contextualization properly so called,
or of contiguity:[22] "It is through the virtue of *Malkhuth* that the
children of Israel deserved to inherit the land, *according to the
terms of the verse*: 'This (*zot*) is the land that shall fall to you as
your portion' (Num. 34:2) [textual foundation],[23] *because* this
virtue is that which dwells on the earth" (*Sha'aré Orah*, p. 28)
(logical-conventional foundation).

Or again, a little further on: "By his benevolence, we accede
to the world to come [logical-conventional foundation] and it
is concerning it that it is said: 'This is the heritage of the servants of the God' (Isa. 54, 17)" (*Sha'aré Orah*, p. 28) (textual foundation).

In this presentation, the reader will have noted a double justification. Moreover, the text goes on: "It is also the specific
virtue of royalty, which Judah has deserved [conventional-
historical foundation], *as this verse says*: 'This [*zot*] he said of Judah' (Deut. 33:7)" (*Sha'aré Orah*, p. 28)[24] (textual foundation).

If Judah, the founder of the royal dynasty in Israel, is on one
hand identified as such with the sphere of *Malkhuth*, which signifies "kingdom," that relation is, on the other hand, based on
the textual juxtaposition of *zot* and *Judah*. This return to the text,
whose precise logical link to the conventional exposition is un-
clear, obviously becomes problematic on the theoretical plane
and offers a point of attachment for multiple interpretations.

In an initial evaluation, which seeks to respect the principle
of organization and the homogeneity of the kabbalistic series,
the text cited might be said to empty itself of its locutionary
force[25] in order to present itself in a static arrangement of sym-

bols. It would then no longer truly function as a text: rather, one could see in it a coded referential field, obtained through the projection of conventional paradigms onto the syntagmatic structure of the Bible.[26]

In this reading, the anagogic networks would thus admit a verbal verification: that of the *contiguity* of terms in the biblical utterance. This contiguity will be comprehended in the broad sense, and proceeds from a poetic form of arrangement of signs. Contrary to the effects of contextualization, the alliances that it produces are *not* subject to the *linguistic process of signification.*

Its inspiration is here again of a symbolic rather than a semiotic order, since the simple juxtaposition of signs suffices (on a first reading) to ensure their appurtenance to a single class, before their combination in the utterance. Ultimately, the coincidence of these syntagmatic environments and the matricial lists of Sod would have to be verified by a computer, not taking into account, in this mechanical operation, the exact (grammatical) arrangement of the terms; here the logic of associations is graphic and related to preestablished networks.

Let us take as an illustration the following verse from Exodus: "Let them make me a Tabernacle that I may dwell among them" (Exod. 25:8). *Sha'aré Orah* bases itself on this utterance in order to deduce a semantic equivalence between "Tabernacle" and "dwell" (or "Presence that dwells"), sememes that are both integrated into the sphere of *Malkhuth* (p. 15).

More generally, it will be considered legitimate, from the point of view of the functioning of the grids, to attach in series the constituents of a single context. Under the name "siman," or indication, the Kabbalah makes abundant use of this reading, as an allusion to underlying proximities. Examples are extremely numerous, even though rarely made explicit as such, and they are based at the same time on a logical argument (or any coded kind of association). However, the distribution of the terms into categories, according to the lists drawn up by the kabbalistic dictionaries, brings out an operational regularity.

"This (*zeh*) shall be my name forever" (Exod. 3:15). This

verse, cited in the fifth chapter of *Sha'aré Orah,* yields the following keys:

- "This" (*zeh*): belongs to the semantic sphere of *Yesod* or *Tifereth*
- "name": *Yesod*
- "age": *Tifereth*

In the same way:

"Remember this (*zeh*) day" (Exod. 13:3).
- "remember": *Yesod*
- "this": *Yesod*
- "day": *Yesod*

"You have been skirting this (*zeh*) hill long enough" (Deut. 2:3).
- "this" (*zeh*): *Yesod*
- "hill": *Yesod*

"This (*zot*) is the sign of the covenant" (Gen. 9:12 and 9:17).
- "This" (*zot*): *Malkhuth*
- "sign": *Yesod*
- "covenant": *Yesod*

"On that very (*zeh*) day Abraham was circumcised" (Gen. 17:26).
- "that" (*zeh*): *Yesod*
- "day": *Yesod*
- "circumcision": *Yesod*

These relations of appurtenance can be mixed, to the extent to which the spheres of reference are themselves in a relationship of complementarity. Moreover, transfers are clearly necessary to ensure that these combinations have a tentacular extension to the whole of the semantic network.

In "This (*zeh*) is the gateway of the Lord, the just will pass through it" (Ps. 118:20), "this" (*zeh*) refers to *Yesod*, as does the term "the just"; between them is intercalated an allusion to *Malkhuth*, by way of the "gateway" that belongs to its paradigm.

Similarly, in "If He protects me on this (*zot*) path I am following" (Gen. 28:20), we can discern the following distribution: "protect": *Malkhuth*; "this" (*zeh*): *Yesod*; "path": *Tifereth* (according to Cordovero).

However, these variations remain homogeneous, and their fluctuations remain coherent, in spite of the increasingly subtle correspondences. Therefore from this point of view one can reread as purely contiguous expressions connecting a determinant and a determined object, of the type already encountered in *zeh hadavar* (this is the word) or *zot haberakhah* (this is the blessing), which juxtapose two units from the same paradigm.

Anagogic interpretation thus *superimposes* on the relationship of *signification*—which itself arrives at coded determinations—a relationship of *juxtaposition*. At least, in both cases the referential derivation in question ultimately ends up at the text, as the supreme authority of signification.

In fact, this ambivalence between two types of textual recognition, one of which proceeds from language as message and the other from language as coded equation,[27] is maintained on the theoretical plane by traditional exegesis. Thus the expression *zot haberakhah* (this is the blessing) participates simultaneously in both cycles, horizontal and vertical, semantic and positional.

Synthesis: The Metalinguistic Level

One might propose to ground these referential points of view in a second phase of the analysis, through an original technique of textual notation understood as metalinguistic, and which would not invalidate the *linear signification* of the supporting quotations, and would make it possible to maintain the *conventional constituent*. A first key to this integration of systems is provided by the peculiarity of the Hebrew language that consists in the absence of the present tense of the copula "to be."

Through this "ellipsis," any contextual juxtaposition is transposable into an autonomous and coherent syntagm: a reinsertion of the verb *to be* transforms the two terms of a purely formal contiguity into an organized semantic proposition. Thus
the turn of phrase "*zot haberakhah*" can represent *both* the projection of the associative pair "*zot, berakhah*" (pertaining to the
same theme of fecundity) and the utterance of a relation of signification: "This is the blessing."

Anagogic interpretation, which restores to words their absolute value, uses this fact to bring the reading to a new level,
which integrates the two preceding modalities by giving biblical discourse the definitional character of a *metalanguage*.

For the Kabbalah, in fact, each term of the Bible, in each of its
occurrences, is used absolutely. All words in the lexicon are the
names of spiritual spheres and, through their mediation, the
names given to the diverse attributes of God.[28] This is true even
of the demonstrative, which is falsely deictic and wholly oriented toward this secret sphere that represents its true reference. It constitutes its appellation, its specific designation. Prior
to any grammaticalization, it is a proper name:[29] "And by the
fact that Israel received this name as its heritage and that this
Sephirah (*Malkhuth*) was devoted to them, they have become
part of the Blessed-be-He and his patrimony. This virtue dwells
continually among them, and when Israel has to enter into the
presence of the Lord, . . . it is this Virtue that places them before Him. That is why the head priest, on the day of the Great
Pardon, enters the Holy of Holies only with it (Lev. 16:3): 'With
zot, Aaron shall enter the sacred precincts'" (*Sha'aré Orah*, p. 28).

"With *zot*," that is, literally, with the attribute (= *Malkhuth*)
of which *zot* is the appellation.

Let us read at this level the verses cited above:

"And it is concerning it (concerning *this Sphere*) that it is said:
'This is what their father said to them as he blessed them' (Gen.
49:28). . . . Without 'that,' whence would have come the blessing?" (*Sha'aré Orah*, p. 28).

An anagogical commentary to which we must restore its precise teaching: "*Zot* is what their father said to them as he blessed

them . . . for without *zot* (that is, without the attribute of *Mal-khuth*), where would the blessing have come from?"

Moreover, the kabbalist goes on: "And it is by it that our master Moses completed the enterprise of blessing, as it is written": (Deut. 33:1) 'And here (*vezot*) is the blessing with which Moses blessed the children of Israel' (*Sha'aré Orah*, p. 28) [literally, it is by *zot* (= *Malkhuth*) that Moses blessed . . .].

Pardes Rimonim recognizes the same nominal principle in the following verse: "That very (*zeh*) day they arrived in the wilderness of Sinai" (Exod. 19:11). That very day: on the specific day of *zeh* (that is, on the day the children of Israel attained the virtue of *zeh* [= *Yesod*]).

An ("essential") substantialization is thus the linguistic mark of Sod, and makes it possible to restore to it the semantic immediacy of a new Peshat as a new textuality.

At the same time, this systematic hypostasis of terms in the language destroys its morphological hierarchy and transcends the functional distinctions between deictic and nominal group, adjective or pronoun. In particular, this mutation in the grammatical status of words renders the traditional syntax of discourse moot and makes it explode into autonomous syntagms. This results in a new division of the text, through which an originary mechanism of signification is unveiled.

Between these "proper names," through the reestablished presence of the verb *to be*, a direct semantic relation is thus established, a sort of literality *stricto sensu*. Its linguistic constitution, which is intermediary between a normally structured discursive form and the dissociated, syntactically inert units of a conventional paradigm, is assimilable to a metalanguage. In other words, for anagogic interpretation, *the Bible functions as a dictionary*.[30]

The demonstrative is now put between quotation marks; "*zeh*" as a proper name is presented *at the same time as its definition*. While representing the *Sephirah*, it designates itself simultaneously in a textual utterance that, taken literally, has a determinative value (see below).

The relation established between the constituents of a given expression is always a relation of equivalence; each verse (and thus each occurrence of the term to be defined) is assumed to be fundamental, a definition in extension, at the same time necessary and sufficient. The simplest illustration of this mechanism can be furnished by the typical example "This (*zot*) is the blessing," which is transformed into the equation *zot = berakhah*, *zot* is "blessing"—whose terms appear inscribed in a single paradigm, that of *Malkhuth*.

That is also the lesson Gemara draws from the verse: "This (*zeh*) is my God, I shall celebrate his splendor": "*zeh* represents the Holy One, blessed-be-He *specifically*" (*Menahoth* 53b).

The Talmud seems here to be based on an underlying reading, inspired by mysticism: "*zeh* is my God" in the sense of "*zeh*" *signifies* "my God."

But this internal inscription can take more complex forms and truly double the immediate reading: "This one (*zot*) *shall be called* woman, for this one (*zot*) was taken from man" (Gen. 2:23).

Anagogy considers this statement as a codified proposition; it associates *zot* with "woman" in a single thematic derivation starting from the sign "man": "*zot* shall receive the name of 'woman' because '*zot*' has [as woman] been (re)taken from 'man.'"[31] In doing so, anagogy marks the stages in an organized recognition of the spheres through the words of the language.

Moreover, tradition recognizes a more marked character, a more comprehensive definition, in the first occurrence of each term in the biblical text. For the Kabbalah, it is indeed in this verse, indicating its first appearance, that the correspondence of *zot* with a semantic trait of femininity is established. This correspondence in turn justifies (and is perhaps grounded in) its primordial appurtenance to the feminine sphere of *Malkhuth* and to the latter's thematic schema of fecundity.

In the same way, Nahmanides pursues his commentary on *zot*[32] by means of this quotation from Psalms: "This (*zot*) came to us from God" (Ps. 118:23): "How do we know that *zot* represents the blessing? We learn it from the verse: 'This (*zot*) came to us from God.'"

Or taken absolutely: *zot* came to us from God. This reading
will be radicalized: *zot* is defined by the fact that it came to us
from God; thus it represents the intervention of Providence: it
is, par excellence, blessing.

Here are other characteristic examples of this level of reading: "By this (*bezoth*) you shall know that I am the Lord" (Exod.
7:17). "The pharoah, tradition teaches us, was more clever than
his magicians, since he perceived this *zot* [that is, the attribute
of *Malkhuth*], and understood that It would punish him, and
destroy his country. Just as Moses had predicted: 'By *zot*, you
shall know that I am the Lord'" (Zohar B 37b or *Bo* 34, 117).

Or, reread absolutely: *zot* is this intervention that manifests
the divine power.

The following verse lends itself to the same type of reading: "For this (*zot*) law which I enjoin upon you is not beyond
your understanding" (Deut. 30:11), letting it be understood that
the Torah is by nature within man's reach, commensurable with
his truth.

Finally, let us cite Jacob's exclamation, when the true *nature*
of the place in which he is lying is revealed to him in a dream,
and whose utterance signifies simultaneously the evidence of
the place and the evidence of the word by which this place is
defined: "This (*zeh*) is none other than the abode of God and
that (*vezeh*) is the gateway to heaven" (Gen. 28:17). In this literal equivalence, *zeh* is presented as "the abode of God" and as
"the gateway to heaven," an equivalence unveiled once again
in the passage from *Yesod* to *Malkhuth*.

This particular phenomenon of hypostasis (or "nominaliza-
tion"), which corresponds in other respects to a precise metaphysical vision, thus confers on biblical discourse the status of
a metatext in which each element of specific utterances is redefined in the linguistic system. A hybrid discourse, proposing
an utterance that is semantically organized but circular and
wholly turned toward the linguistic system that subtends it.

The Kabbalah reduces this double orientation to a unique
form of expression. The two modalities are not only compatible but merged in a single structure, that of a metalanguage,
which expresses simultaneously the code and the combination

of its units.[33] At this level of interpretation the biblical text thus conveys in each case a double load of information, whose ambiguity is constitutive.

As a proper term, a divine name, each word of the Torah is defined by its absolute reference, its coded correspondence with the *Sephirah* it represents. But at the same time, it is caught up in a context of determination that proposes a linguistic substitute for it. What the Bible *aligns* in its discourse is the series of *paradigmatic* references codified by Sod. That is why the ensemble of the determinations in context normally coincides with the ensemble of the thematic projections of each sphere. This functional identity will have repercussions on exegetical procedure. Here again, the (methodological) orientation of semanticization remains open, the axes of reference remain permutable. In particular, the relations of equivalence inscribed in the very flesh of the text make it possible to choose each biblical term in turn as "unknown" or as determinant.[34]

We now understand better the weight of ambiguity borne by the traditional formulas of both talmudic and kabbalistic midrash: "as it is said," or "as it is written," and so on, are expressions that bring every interpretation back to the final canon of the text, halfway between a proof that establishes and an illustration that makes explicit. Interpretation, in deploying its registers, always starts from an utterance so as to come back and run up against it. No theoretical credo defines the dividing line between the textual presuppositions and the conventional a priori assumptions.

Functional transitivity thus takes over from categorial transitivity, to express the interweaving of the code and the message, of the systematic and the contingent. Signification is a symbolism, but the symbols obey the laws of the text. In the square of possible referentializations, which we shall schematize by the diagram shown on page 141, is expressed, vertically, the correspondence between connotation and analogy that makes it possible, by crossing the successive levels of interpretation, to connect the truths of the text with cosmic truths. Horizontally, this correspondence expresses the parallel constitution of these universes, opening a fixed and ritualized rela-

CODED LEVEL

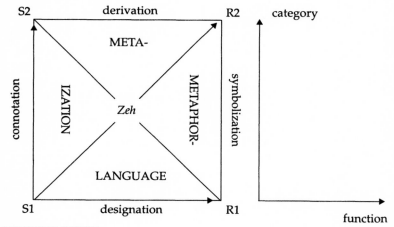

TEXTUAL LEVEL

tionship onto indeterminable textual play and unpredictable subjectivities.

At the same time, the midrashic perspective, which is oriented toward the semantic expectations of the Kabbalah, also makes it possible to diffract and multiply these complexes on distinct levels of experience by elaborating them in the psychical or moral concreteness of the biblical narrative.

Ultimately, the set of references associated with any term whatever in the text can emanate simultaneously from that term, along with the set of the functionings of sense by which these references are deduced. Each term is the nucleus of a constellation of forms and contents, of functions and signs in continual equivalence, in an equilibrium of substitution.

SUPERIMPOSITIONS

This confusion of signs, and of the semiotic orders that bear them, explains the difficulty encountered in practice when trying to isolate differentiated principles of sense. Usually, in fact, and because of the homologous status of the techniques of derivation, a sort of methodological indeterminacy is established in the details of the exegesis. To complete its itinerary, the effort to elucidate each term passes from one scale to another, like an acrobat on trapezes.

Without noticing them, the Kabbalah or the Midrash carry along these irreconcilable networks in a single wave, and ground them reciprocally. To make this kind of centrifugal/centripetal organization clearer, we have sought to bring together in a single diagram several commentaries grouped around a single verse. The continuous study of these midrashim ultimately sets into place a unique sphere of signification, constructed around the generic theme-term *zot*. It is evident that this diagram constructed according to our perspective (focused on the use of the demonstrative) could also pivot on any of its terms. On the schema must appear conjointly, in the interweaving of the themes, the plurality of the demonstrations *and* the regularity of the series. In this "garden of forking paths" sense moves forward in a manner that is both undecided and determined.

The nucleus verse chosen, whose echo is already familiar, is drawn from Genesis: "All these were the tribes of Israel, twelve in number, and it is thus that their father spoke to them and blessed them, giving to each the blessing appropriate to him" (Gen. 49:28).

Mystical Identification

The term *zot*, as we know, is systematically connected by anagogy with the *Sephirah* of *Malkhuth*. That is the option taken by *Sha'aré Orah* in interpreting the occurrence of the demonstrative in our verse.

Example I

"And it is of it [= the *Sephirah* of *Malkhuth*] that it is said: 'And it is thus (*vezot*) that their father spoke to them and blessed them'" (*Sha'aré Orah*, p. 28).

This conventional correlation respects a thematic coherence that makes of *Malkhuth*, the last of the spheres, the source of all blessing. In the Kabbalah's conception, it explains the presence of *zot* in this context where Jacob asks divine mercy for his children.

Example II

"The man who wants to praise the King is permitted to do so only through the attribute of Presence [*Shekhinah*, one of the manifestations of *Malkhuth*], as it is said in the verse: 'That is why (*al zot*) every pious man must pray to you' (Ps. 32:6), that is, pray only through *zot* (= *Malkhuth*). Now Jacob knew that the King's will passed through this Attribute; he thus advised his children to present themselves before Him only with it, as it is written: 'And it is thus [*vezoth*, that is, *Malkhuth*] their father spoke to them and blessed them'" (*Tikkuné Zohar*, 6).[35]

Through its conventional structuring, this recognition of *zot* as equivalent to *Malkhuth* opens in turn onto all the harmonics of its "theme," among which we shall note (anticipating the complementary midrashim) Presence (or Providence, translating the Hebraic term *Shekhinah*), the Torah, and of course— Blessing.[36]

INTERTEXTUALITY

Midrash links this verse, by contextual memorization (see chapter 3), with the blessing given by Moses to Israel on the eve of his death, and which begins with the same term *zot*.

Example III

"How did Jacob carry out his blessing? With the word *zot*, as is shown in the text of the verse: 'And it is thus [*vezoth*] that their father spoke to them and blessed them.' And when Moses was ready to bless the children of Israel, he wanted to begin only with this same *zot*. Whence do we get it? From what the verse tells us: 'Now here is [*vezoth*] the blessing with which Moses, the man of God, blessed the children of Israel before he died' (Deut. 33:1)" (*Midrash Rabbah*, Deut. 11:1).

In accordance with an already noted procedure, the recurrence of the word *zot* leads to a comparison of the contexts in which it appears. However, this textual equation operates at several levels:

- The precise return of the term *zot* in a relationship of contiguity-contextuality with the repeated idea of "blessing" leads to the identification of the contents, in their profound resonance. In its distinct versions, it is in fact the same specific blessing that is drawn out from the founding Fathers to the legislator Moses.

- A more exact examination of the order of the terms in each context makes it possible to inscribe the Mosaic blessing in the direct wake of Jacob's, and literally as its *prolongation*. Thus Moses repeats word for word the prophecy of the patriarch, at the very point where the latter had interrupted it: at the word *zot*.

- Finally, this intertextuality can be interpreted in a broad sense as the encounter of two thematic ensembles. The connection of one occurrence of *zot* to another makes it possible to align in a single continuity the historical authority (Jacob blessing his children) and the moral authority (Moses blessing his disciples).

These different perspectives, opened up on the basis of a single textual equivalence, are indicated in a second, more complete version of the same midrash.

Example IV

"'And it is thus [*vezoth*] that their father spoke to them': A man who resembles me is called to bless you one day, and to take up this blessing at the point where I interrupted it" (*Midrash Rabbah*, Gen. 100:12).

"And in fact, when Moses was ready to bless Israel, he began with the expression: 'This is [*vezoth*] the blessing,' repeating the very terms with which their father Jacob had concluded" (*Sifré, Vezoth Haberakhah*, 1). "'And it is thus [*vezoth*] that their father spoke to them': When will these blessings take effect? On the day you accept the Torah, in which it is written '*vezoth ha-*

torah' (And here is the Torah)" (*Midrash Rabbah*, Gen. 100:12). (See also *Tanhumah, Vayehi* 17.)

In addition to the deductions of intertextuality already cited, there is also in this more complete version a new derivation (the derivation of "Torah"), linked to this context (Moses' *blessing*) through a third occurrence of *zot*, in the appeal made to the quotation from Deuteronomy: "And here is (*vezoth*) the Torah," where *zot* reappears and is semanticized this time as "Torah."

NUMERICAL CALCULATION
(MIDRASH AND SOD)

We shall put under this rubric two very different examples of commentaries, still on the same verse. In both it will be noted that the numerical calculation, which is in each case founded on a distinct type of operation, is itself interpreted and connected with a known semantic identification.

Example V

"'All these are the twelve tribes of Israel: and it is thus (*vezoth*) that their father spoke to them and blessed them'; if we add to the twelve tribes of Israel the value represented by the term *zot*, we arrive at the number 13 [which is traditionally the symbolic number of the divine Presence, or *Shekhinah*]. Thus divine Presence has come to join them, making it possible for the blessings to be carried out." (Zohar C 62a or *Aharé Moth* 36, 107).

This is not a very mathematical calculation, and above all reinforces, by repeating it in numbers, the conventional identification of *zot* with the *Shekhinah*.

Example VI

An unusual exegete, Ba'al Haturim,[37] rediscovers as well, through the method of gematria with which he is familiar, an equivalence of numbers and letters by which "*zot*" and "blessing" are connected with "Torah" (in this case it is the verse announcing Moses' blessing that is directly referred to):

"'Now here is [*vezoth*] the blessing': in its numerical value, this expression is equivalent to this other one: 'Such is the Torah.' To tell us that Moses blessed them by the merit of the Torah." (Ba'al Haturim, *Vezoth Haberakhah*, Deut. 33:1).

HALAKHA (RITUAL LEGISLATION)

We have sought to integrate into this hermeneutic the midrashim oriented toward the code of concrete behaviors, or Halakhah. If, as we have claimed, Midrash (-*Aggada*) itself represents the existential projection of archetypal paradigms, we enter with the *Midrash Halakhah* into the particular jurisprudence of everyday life.

As a metaphysical possibility, this passage from the symbolic to the ritual is interesting in itself, and will be taken up again in the Conclusion. What we want to observe here is the procedure followed by the decision makers, and, yet again, the insertion of their analyses into an overall thematic program.

Example VII

"The priest who commits an error in uttering a prayer yields his place to another. At what point in the text must the latter begin? At the beginning of the blessing in which the first priest made a mistake. We draw this lesson from the example of the patriarchs. Each of them in fact began his blessing at the point where his predecessor had interrupted it. . . . How did Jacob conclude his? By *zot*, just as it is written: 'And it is thus [*vezot*] that their father spoke.' And when Moses was ready to bless the children of Israel, he wanted to begin only with this same '*zot*' . . . " (*Midrash Rabbah*, Deut. 11:1).

Here we must note the *literal* character of the reading, which transposes the syntagmatic order of the narrative into the corresponding ritual structure. At the same time, the thematic contextualization is respected: it is indeed the *blessing* that trips up the reciter.[38]

To mark, beneath its diversity, the cohesion of this ensemble among others,[39] we shall redraw, with its branchings, the following hermeneutic tree.

Genesis 49:28
"And it is thus that their father spoke to them and blessed them."

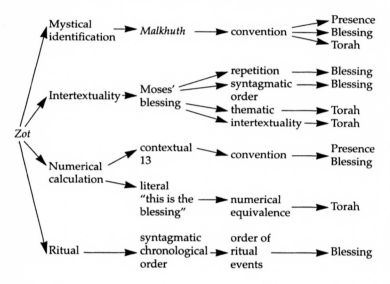

From this it emerges forcefully that beneath the pointillism of each commentary taken in itself, the appearance of arbitrariness is merely an effect of any isolated reading; the network looms in the background. We thus come back to a principle brought out in the introduction, which underlies both the spirit and the practice of commentary: conventional, contextual, or existential, every exegetic utterance is caught between these contradictory poles of multiple movement and necessary conclusion, precision and freedom. Midrash explodes an initial mystical notion into several narratives, illustrating the concurrent paths of actualization. Inversely, textual sources that are distinct and separately apprehended converge toward the same fundamental significations.[40] The determinate kabbalistic structure is infinitely extendable through midrashic plurivalence, which extends it in a dialectic—which is sometimes reversed—of the theme and its variations.

The paradox is explained, on the methodological plane, by new forms of reading, which place at their keystone a general transitivity of criteria. What is presented as theoretical ambiguity, and leaves open the debate concerning the textual norm and the exegete's freedom, is in the end a controlled disparity. And the latter no doubt has the best claim to be representative of the particular tradition of Jewish hermeneutics.

These ambivalences show clearly enough to what point biblical language presented itself to the Sages in its perfection, in a sort of totalizing dream in which freedom and exactitude would not be contradictory. From the philosophical point of view, there is in this a very refined "mathematical" sensibility that allows a principle of uncertainty in which movement and regulation coexist.

At differing degrees of explicitness or integration of systems, the lines are laid down for an intersectional play between the words of the truth and the stakes of interpretation. The ludic facet is illuminated in diverse ways, and its relationship to the absolute is more or less sensed.

In the course of these reversals a belief in unity that exceeds the exegetical arena persists. It posits at the level of being a "philosophy of ambiguity" divided between energy and matter, between rightness and reality. If this squaring of the "hermeneutic circle" is possible, it is because the world in mutation is itself the project of an origin, a historical adventure necessarily turning on the essential.

The osmosis of meanings thus reproduces a deeper, ontological harmony. In the conclusion we shall examine the articulations by means of which this logic of words returns to its source, toward a logic of things.

Conclusion

The compatibility recognized in the preceding chapters goes beyond the accidents of a general confusion of signs, of a dull thud in which the correspondence among the systems, and, at the heart of each system, the combination of their units, would be muted.

This ultimate coincidence of the text and the symbol, which corresponds to the Jewish hermeneutic genius, is inscribed within a broader cosmic order of which it represents only one phase. This cosmic harmony deploys, in a structuration that is simultaneously complex and strongly hierarchized, the initial emanation of the Light-without-end spread over things. In this semioticized universe, in a way that will be clarified, the sequence of successive enclosures bends back within itself—and turns around and prolongs—diverse modes of representation that proceed uncertainly, stumbling on the letters but always passing through the text, from the most spiritual to the most concrete, from the truths that elude us to the objects that we touch.

The image we shall give of this overall organization can only be crude and misleading. Abandoning the hope of rendering its extreme subtlety and infinite resonances, we shall present, in a very simplifying manner, merely a fundamental principle of composition.[1] The latter will nevertheless suffice, by its double nature, to explain and subsume phenomena of ambivalence previously encountered.

THE FUNDAMENTAL MODULES

The Kabbalah recounts, in an atemporal chronology that makes the "times" of being and the modes of its substance correspond, the logic of the successive emanations whereby the reality—internal or manifest—of the created world will be engendered. This cosmogony, which is very difficult to grasp, is initially presented as a hierarchy of values, generating, on the basis of an original Infinite, the emanation of a Light that descends from universe to universe, without any interruption,[2] down to the humbleness of the earth.

After the initial *contraction* by which the Infinite gave *place* to the world,[3] the overflowing of the initial Light takes on a double brilliance, according to whether it still emanates directly—in a straight line, says the Kabbalah (*kav yashar*)—from the original radiation or proceeds from that residual brilliance (*reshimu*) that it left behind it in its withdrawal. It thus hollows itself out inwardly into a space that suggests the receptive modality of the creature.[4]

For the whole of the created world, the very principle of all existence is divided according to this double disposition of the Light given or received, making fecund or diminished, which contains in germ the ontological—and moral—ambivalence of all the worlds to come.

The more the Light "descends," the more it encounters and fills, from within itself, this wish-to-receive that broadens. At the origin of its flowing forth, the radiation is altogether offering, profusion. At the lowest point of its trajectory, it is almost entirely dulled by the thickness of the receptacles that absorb its brilliance.

In this manner is elaborated, according to the relative proportion of saving or hidden Light, through the universe as a whole and traversing each universe, a scale of the derivations that issue from the *Ein Sof*, the absolute Infinite, and urging toward existence five successive worlds:

1. *Adam Kadmon*, or First being[5]
2. *Aziluth*, or Emanation
3. *Beriyah*, or Creation
4. *Yetzirah*, or Fashioning
5. *Asiyah*, or Action, which corresponds to the perceivable universe.[6]

The originary *Ein Sof* is irreducible to the order of the universe and is radically separated, by the emptying-out of its Light, from the principle of all ulterior creation. It is nevertheless linked with it by the emanation of rays of light projected toward the lower worlds (*Kav Yashar*). For their part, these rays of light as a remainder, as memory of absence, as puddles of light, gradually grow thicker, from world to world, in order to make themselves into dust, a material substance.

The radically originary *Adam Kadmon* represents the universe's space of possibility, its luminous *project*. In the world of the *Aziluth*, which is truly primary and anterior to the living, light and receptacle merge, in that light is living and the receptacle is translucent, melted into it. It is only starting with the *Beriyah* that the *kelim*, or utensils or recipients, are distinguished, delimiting the light and drinking it in, with progressive degrees of filtering.[7]

This general configuration of the worlds, established in accordance with the criterion of a transparency and a photogenics—cosmic names given to the necessary and dialectical cycle of all fecundity—presents the completed point of view of a static and differentiated scale. The Kabbalah puts in correspondence with it a base-10 division that divides up the universe as a totality into ten spiritual spheres, mediations between the Creating and the created. These mediations are perceived in relation to the divine attribute that founds them, as general modalities of being. In this respect, they realize the structuration not only of the world as a whole but also of each element it contains. In the image of the Creation, every living cell is broken down into ten complementary and ordinal functions.

These ten *Sephirot* are the ones we encountered in chapter 3:[8]

1. *Keter* (Crown)
2. *Hokhmah* (Wisdom)
3. *Binah* (Intelligence)
4. *Hesed* (Mercy)
5. *Gevurah* (Judgment)
6. *Tifereth* (Splendor)
7. *Nezah* (Eternity)

8. *Hod* (Majesty)
9. *Yesod* (Foundation)
10. *Malkhuth* (Kingdom).[9]

They are regrouped, according to internal relationships that make it possible to bring six of them together under the aegis of *Tifereth*, in five fundamental dimensions (corresponding in a

The *Sephiroth*		The worlds
Keter		Adam Kadmon
Hokhmah		Aziluth
Binah		Beriyah
Hesed Geuurah Tifereth Nezah Hod Yesod	Tifereth	Yetzirah
Malkhuth		Asiyah

diptych to the five primordial registers of the universe).

This division forms a mobile grid of interpretation that accommodates itself to the scope of the reality onto which it is projected. It is thus found indicating the Creation as well as the particular worlds that compose it and then the subunits into which the latter are in turn analyzed:

> Just as each particular world is subdivided into ten *Sephirot*, the totality of the worlds is divided into ten generic Spheres. (*Maftehei Hokhmahta Ha'emeth*, siman 12)

> As for the details of this structuration, it must be recognized that not only does each of the four worlds reproduce the division of the ten *Sephiroth*, but each of their elements, even the tiniest, breaks down in turn into these same ten *Sephiroth*. (Rabbi Ashlag, Preface to the Zohar, p. 95)

This classification, in the simplified versions (generally base 4 or base 5), is itself repeated according to different functional models, which are so many possible apprehensions of the universe. One of them proposes a theory of knowledge involving a scale of four distinct factors of perception: the essence (*Malkhuth*), the form (*Zurah*), the impression of the form on matter (*Zurah hamelubesheth bahomer*), and matter (*homer*).

The first modality is that of the Unknowable, of the In-Itself, the ungraspable, which Hebrew calls *Mahuth*, "essence," the very being of Being. It is, in a specific way—but it is also found in each part of the universe—the modality of the *Ein Sof*, of the Infinite giving its light, which is by itself in its plenitude.

The second modality is that of the form, the active and productive principle, which is first grasped in its abstraction. It is in the world of the *Aziluth* that this germ—this energy to be redistributed on an order of substance, to make it fecund—is unveiled.

In the inferior registers of *Beriyah*, *Yetzirah*, and *Asiyah*, form becomes perceptible to us by shaping matter, working it, giving a name to the space it delimits and which gives it its setting: "This manifestation of essence in the world of phenomena we shall designate by the term 'substance,' or 'matter, 'body,' or 'receptacle. . . . ' As for the passage of the divine light through the prism (of the *Beriyah*), it illustrates the covering of matter by form" (Preface to the Zohar, p. 97).[10]

This approach to the world, which marks the forms and the limits of our comprehension, is thus simultaneously the (constitutive) procedure of all knowledge and applies to every entity, to every object, down to the most concrete, down to our own human identity:

> And it must be repeated that we do not have access to the modality of essence, the modality of the hidden, buried in things, down to this world. (Preface to the Zohar, p. 98, par. 17)
>
> We cannot in any way accede to the level of essence. (Preface, 97, par. 16)
>
> We must remember here that the very being of all reality is at the beginning of essence (*Mahuth*); the latter remains ungraspable for us even in its most concrete manifestations, and even in our own identity. (Preface to the Zohar, p. 99, par. 23)

The most immediate environment thus remains secret, withdrawn, as does Essence itself on the superior plane. As light renewed manifests its "idea" coming down to us, in the same way, at any level, all truth is perceptible only through the obscuring layer of substance by which it takes on body.

The play of divisions and regroupings, of subdivisions into classes and correspondences, allows multiple conversions from one system to another, from the dynamic to the static and from the general to the particular. The orientations presented are grouped together in the general schema on page 155.

This is a classical but dynamic classification, in that it constantly slips over itself and makes itself available to numerous symbolic transpositions. According to the allegorical perspective elected, this same arrangement will have new avatars by playing alternately with the letters of the alphabet and with those of the Tetragrammaton, the levels of the soul, the parts of the body or those of the face, colors, moral virtues, and so on.[11]

These preliminaries will prepare us to enter into the logic of the structuration and interaction of the worlds.

THE STRUCTURING OF THE WORLDS

LINEAR SCHEMA

The diagram below is in fact global and perfectly linear. This movement by which the superior "meaning" inspires the reality of concrete visions, this luminous dynamism of Creation, can be assimilated in a metaphorical fashion[12] to a referential function: from the most ethereal, virtual project of the creature-to-come to the carnal clay of the concrete universe, it is always the same Light, in its permanence, that traverses these lenses, these prisms, that grow thicker and thicker. The particular name of each object is given by the *encounter* between this luminous influx and the call of being—the receptacle—that has proceeded toward it. This superior irradiation "continuously illuminates the lower worlds, just as it illuminates the first and Infinite source, and in the same manner. The transforma-

Dialectic of the Created	The worlds	The *Sephiroth*	Modalities of perception
Light of the Infinite	*Adam Kadmon*	*Keter*	essence
ray of light / trace	*Aziluth*	*Hokhmah*	form
Light / receptacles	*Beriyah*	*Binah*	Form imprinted on matter /
	Yetzirah	*Tifereth*	
	Asiyah	*Malkhuth*	matter

tions are produced only at the level of the receptacles themselves, and retain its expansiveness in proportion to their own (diversified) capacity to receive" (Rabbi Ashlag, *Sefer Hahakdamoth*, "Talmud Eser Sephiroth," chap. 2, p. 46).

There is thus a crystallization, an *actualization*, of a new sense at the intersection of each will to be and this primordial energy that filters through it.[13] Like the sense, the Light "that has fallen from the firmament" remains self-identical and precipitates, in a particular reference, a given spiritual "object," according to the *context* that it brings to life.

The Kabbalah underscores this kind of structure through the already-cited image of the prism, in a precise symbolics of colors:

> The Zohar relates these ten *Sephiroth* to four fundamental colors, which are white for *Hokhmah*, red for *Binah*, green for *Tifereth*, and black for *Malkhuth* (A 16a or Gen. 34:22). . . .
> This correspondence can be explained by the image of a prism with four facets, tinted in accord with these four colors. And although the light that passes through them is one, it is colored in passing through the prisms and diffracted in several reflections: white, red, green, or black light. Thus the original

brilliance that irradiates all the *Sephiroth* is divine and undivided, from the project of the superior world of the *Aziluth* to the completion, at the lowest level, of the world of the *Asiyah*. But this subdivision into ten *Sephiroth* proceeds from the receptacles' wish to receive, and it is in passing through them, like a fine membrane, that light seems to modify its color, as a function of each specific tint.

(Rabbi Ashlag, Preface to the Zohar, p. 95, par. 7)

Thus objects apprehend the Light from the angle of their particular aim.

CONCENTRIC SCHEMA

But alongside or within the limits of this "functional" and generic organization, which lays down the stages of a unique system of reference that unfolds vertically the repetitive formation of its units, the Kabbalah also recognizes an internal structuration that breaks up each world, each level of being taken in itself. This transverse section reveals ("synchronic") relations rather than differences of level properly so called.

In all cases, the principle of a sort of microcosmic, analogical reproduction of the general order of the created, in each instant in which its movement is fixed, is established. The simple line of emanation or derivation of the spheres is in fact a partition or parturition, an engendering of itself from within, an enclosure of the worlds fitted one inside the other which give birth to one another: "We know that the *Sephiroth* are enclosed within each other, and that six of them, from *Keter* to *Malkhuth*, are framed within the *Sephira* of *Keter*, and in the same way ten within *Hokhmah*, and ten within *Tifereth* and *Malkhuth*" (Preface to the Zohar, p. 104, par. 39).

This infinite subdivision redistributes the elements of Creation in a relationship that is no longer actual and differentiated in accord with each "context," but which echoes, from stratum to stratum, a recurrent representation of the symbols included in each universe. We will set these two techniques of description side by side in the schema on page 157.

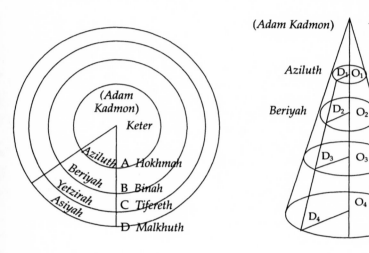

Schema I (actualization)

Schema II (analogy)

STRUCTURAL AMBIVALENCE

These two schemas normally represent two points of view of the same configuration. The first graph, which shows the overall disposition of the elements in question, clearly marks the ambiguity of their structuration. The concentric circles normally represent differences in level, since the luminous flow "descends" from the superior worlds toward the inferior ones. However, at the same time this continuous line crosses the field of possible crystallizations "crosswise" and organizes the different points along a single horizontal axis: A, B, C, D mark not only a scale of values, a shimmering of colors in kabbalistic terminology, but also a combination of elements, a system of relationships, on the basis of a luminous central point opening on all forms of determination.

This horizontal division is repeated at each level of being in Schema II, which allows us to make its units correspond vertically through the superimposition of these mimetic structures:

"It thus becomes clear that the receptacles borne by the ten *Sephiroth* of the inferior worlds receive their vital influx from the homologous *Sephira* in the world of *Aziluth*. Thus each element actualized corresponds to its virtual principle in the 'program' of the superior levels" (Preface to the Zohar, p. 101, par. 28).

This structural ambivalence recalls and confirms transitivities discovered in the preceding chapter. It establishes the concomitance, if not the actual equivalence, of a static analogical division oriented toward the "code" and a dynamic, differential formation on the basis of a single principle, making the intonation of its "message" vary.

Each point in the universe is determined at the same time, *and by the same equation*, in relation to the ray that it diffracts and in relation to the homologous point that corresponds to it in another sphere. In it merge, in linguistic terms, a level of sense and a referential determination.

The convergences revealed above, which put in competition contradictory forms of derivation and heterogeneous relations among systems, thus here find their end, and at the same time a sort of ontological foundation. First of all, it appears in fact that here again the paradigm of the ten spheres is projected onto the syntagm of the world in development. The levels of being, successively traversed by the creative ray of light, arrange themselves in accordance with the initial "sephirotic" configuration. The process of events inscribes secretly calculated gaps within the space of the living; it develops, in the very history of its advent, the schema of its deep destiny.

This folding back of a vertical axis onto the horizontal axis is complicated further by an internal iconicity: at the same time that it is deployed according to its specific rhythm, the movement of creation reproduces it at each level of its cycle. Caught at regular intervals along the path of light, each point of being unveils, within its very unity, the organization into ten spheres that is constitutive of all reality.

Whatever field of reality is considered, the linear relation that unites any two points is thus simultaneously intrasystematic and intersystematic. It is intrasystematic in that each unit is integrated into the general design of the spheres, in a precise fraction; and it is intersystematic to the extent that this very arrangement is always analogical, translated from one plane to another. The location of a reference is coded; but it also becomes a symbolic relation between two codes.

Time remakes space, the universe in process is always moving forward, toward its own *mise en abyme*, which represents both its initial structure and the stages of its formation. The cycle of the world "bites its own tail" in coming into the world. This complex organicity, which bears the mergings of meaning, explains its continual vibration in hermeneutics.[14] The convergence of the reference points of signification comes from farther back and is inscribed against the background of the harmony of cosmic constellations.

THE ONTOLOGICAL
METAPHOR OF LANGUAGE

In the generation of the values of being, the order of language appears as homologous in turn and constitutively modeled on the order of the world. As we have said, the text—the labyrinthine paths of meaning—is only a new modality, another unveiling of this unique underlying structure.

THE COSMOS AND WRITING

After the Midrash, the Kabbalah perceives the allegory of this underlying structure in the form of an inverted relationship: the Kabbalah infers, on the basis of a symbolics of writing, the subterranean alchemy of the universe:[15] "The superior brilliances take the name of 'book,' according to the expression of the *Sefer Yetzirah* (chap. 1, mishnah 1): 'He created his universe by three modalities of writing: the book, the writer, and the written'" (quoted in the Preface to the Zohar, p. 96, par. 8).

Or a little further on: "The four worlds A B Y A[16] constitute the 'book of heaven'—a white background marked with three colors of ink, in which we recognize the characteristic hues of the three inferior worlds" (Preface to the Zohar, p. 96, par. 8).

This metaphor of the cosmos and writing, which is presupposed by the ideology as well as by the methodology (since the laws of meaning reinsert and recompose themselves in those of the world), sounds familiar to the contemporary ear. Many data confirm the pertinence of the transposition, which puts the *semiosis* of the world into conformity with that of language.

This symmetry is first precisely established by the theoretical orientation of the Kabbalah. The latter apprehends—on its lighted side, the only one accessible to reading—a Creation that addresses itself to man and culminates in him. It is in their relation to man, and as perceived by a consciousness, that the spheres are organized in their fragmentation: "the reader must understand that the elements of the superior worlds in question are grasped only in the precise degree that they concern the soul of man . . . so that the name of the Infinite does not refer to the intrinsic reality of the Eternal, but to the *relationship established*, through this designation, to the Creation and its creatures" (Preface to the Zohar, p. 99, par. 23). This phenomenological anthropocentrism emerges at the same time in a philosophy of absence that organizes the signs into systems of negativities.[17]

"DIFFERENCE"

The very existence of the world is based on the initial withdrawal of the In-itself, creation becoming possible in the yawning gap of a contracted Light, reality modeling itself in the very distance that separates it from the initial source of all reality: "It is in being torn away from its light, that the receptacle accedes to itself" (Rabbi Ashlag, "Introduction to the Kabbalah," *Sefer Hahakdamoth*, p. 114, par. 14).

Thus the existent is defined by the very thing that is *taken* away from it in order to make it exist. This initial withdrawal that founds our condition itself is not a destruction but an occultation.[18] However, everything that participates in the essential Light is apprehended in the form of the hidden: we can grasp only a diffuse manifestation[19] in the material *operations* in which it is incarnated.[20]

What remains between our fingers is a vibration, the perception of a relationship. All matter is composed of atoms, all emanation signifies a combination of units. It is the latter's complexity that marks the distance between the created and the first Absolute. Beyond that impossibility of the origin looms a necessary identification of reality and structure, or, to resort to Saussurean terminology,[21] a "negative" definition of the element by its "value" in the system. To be sure, this "double articulation"[22] of the cosmic order comes back to an ideology of *relation* as the only being possible, a sort of relativist equation between position and nature that an orthodox structuralist of the 1960s would not have disavowed.

RELATION AND PLENITUDE

However, we must reject the philosophical conclusions to be drawn from this temptation to amalgamate. For if all reality in fact scintillates in a precise point in the economy of the spheres, it is "caught up" at the same time in the luminous flow that makes worlds rise up. It is indeed at the intersection of *two* lights, that of the receptacle and that of the influx, that the element is fashioned and takes on body. The exchange of essence and function is ambivalent. If the kabbalistic program can be read on a computer, it also presupposes a play of *substances*.

Already in its elementary vertical arrangement, the Kabbalah "does not represent being but passage," the same light is always called out in its different refractions. The multiplicity of the created is a shadow projected by an internal aim, the dispersed sign of a hidden reality.

And yet, for the kabbalistic sensibility these reflections, these forms, which are the residual *trace* of a lost brilliance, do not merely dance illusorily on the wall of a fabled cavern: the ray of light that still filters through the opacity of unsatisfied desires, the thin thread that has *come back* to us after the withdrawal of a sun to the zenith, continues to bear, even in the crudest matter, the first essence, inalienable and perpetuated by the original Light; by the supreme, superior Light of this primitive and absolute incandescence, which is the vital principle of everything that comes into being: "the light of the superior regions has not been reduced by the 'withdrawal' of the Infinite, nor has it been altered; its brilliance remains intact, before and after it, permanently in all the worlds."[23]

And thus the recognition of the system is at the same time an intuition of the essence, the presence (even if occulted) of being, self-identical from its source.

Now, each object, which is only a point in the arrangement of the spheres, expresses simultaneously the degree of radiation that traverses it at its particular site, and the imprint of the Value that corresponds to it, when it is arranged from the same angle and offers itself to the same light, somewhere "ahead" in the project of creation, at the dawn of all will: "Even in its smallest details, the reality of the created world follows the design of the initial Infinite" (Preface to the Zohar, p. 100, par. 26).

In this double process of engendering is revealed a still deeper organic, circular link between the "high" and the "low," between dream and matter, between a primordial concept and the concrete form through which the latter is realized. The structure of an atomic nucleus is repeated from world to world, projected and found again in each world, and each time close to itself.

FROM THE LIGHT TO THE LIGHT

The existential principle of faith, according to which "in the achievement of the actual relation the intention is unveiled at its origin,"[24] is thus also applicable to the order itself of the worlds, conceived as an infinite homological derivation, the maturation of an original seed, already bearing all the programs of being to come. For if the universe of men represents the ultimate end of a desire to give being, if it is at the same time as a maximum distancing in relation to a point of origin, a radical exile, an extreme condensation of light into matter, it is also, going back to the source, the inverted image of the ineffable project in its initial, most intimate, most evanescent interiority. The signs are inverted, but the numbers remain identical in absolute value. What is most distant is at the same time the closest, the original emanation comes back toward itself, in contradiction with itself. What impurities there are in the human clay, what makes it heavy and sticky, is the weight of this waiting, which marks it with the Creator's seal. Void and plenitude thus ceaselessly exchange their exponents.[25]

And thus the most ephemeral breath of our life is the most freighted with eternity, the opaque matter of the event is the most pregnant with living light. At each one of our steps, a tumult of truths rises up.[26]

And it is here again, one last time, the same sign of evidence, the paradox begun over again, of an absolute inscribed in matter, and which extends itself in it. The Light is dimmed, but not put out, by the act that obscures it. All degradation of a fallen morality is ontologically called on to reverse itself.[27] That is why the meticulous system of the eternal verities is compatible with the irrepressible movement of History. That is why the coded meaning is borne by the breath of a specific utterance. All functioning, even anarchical, withdraws within the bounds of a rule, and Revelation allows itself to be perceived in the form of a pronoun. The word on its way toward its freedom was *foreseen* from the beginning,[28] moving toward a calculable but unexplored unknown, arbitrary though exact. Thus morality takes risks without being lost, tomorrow is foreign to us, but already saved. This world can be taken on, says the memory of Israel, for this world comes back to itself in moving away from itself.

Notes

INTRODUCTION

1. *Midrash Rabbah*, ed. A. M. Mirkin (Tel Aviv: Yavneh, 1968), Gen. 1:10. All quotations from *Midrash Rabbah* will cite this edition.

2. *Avoth*, 6, 2. The Mishnah is divided into treatises (*massekhtoth*), chapters (*perakim*), and sections (*mishnayoth*).

3. *Yerushalmi, pe'ah, perek 2, halakhah 6*. The Jerusalem Talmud, which follows the Mishnah's division of the text, retains notation by chapters (*perakim*) and sections (*halakhoth*), in contrast with the Babylon Talmud, which is classically referred to by page numbers.

4. See especially chap. 1.

5. Mishnah, *Pesahim* 10, 5.

6. In its most common use, the word *midrash* designates an exegesis that goes beyond the literal sense toward secondary interpretations. When the word refers to a particular midrash it will not be capitalized. For a more detailed discussion, see supra, n. 3.

7. See, for example, *Nedarim* 22b; *Gittin* 60b; *Midrash Rabbah*, Exod. 47:1. "If Israel had not sinned, it would have received *only* the Pentateuch and the Book of Joshua" (*Nedarim* 22b). [The rest would have been preserved in the form of oral tradition.] "Rabbi Yohanan taught: the largest part of the Torah is oral, the smaller part is written" (*Gittin* 60b) [This inverts the terms of the one defended by a head rabbi, R. Elazar.] "Rabbi Yohanan taught: the Holy One, blessed-be-He struck an alliance with Israel only for the sake of the Oral Law" (*Gittin* 60b) "What Moses learned from the mouth of the Holy One, blessed-be-He, asked him to teach in turn to Israel. . . . 'Master of the world,' Moses said, 'why not put this teaching in writing?' And He replied: 'Because of the idolators to whom they will be subjected. . . . The Oral Law will serve as their sign and particularity" (*Midrash Rabbah*, Exod. 47:1). In the same chapter, the midrash proposes other interpretations on this theme of the partition into written law and oral law. One of the key verses for this kind of reflection, which is often cited, occurs in Hosea (8:12): "Shall I put the principles of my teaching in writing for him?"

8. *Tanhuma*, Gen. 1. See also Rashi (see chap. 1, n. 39) on Deuteronomy 33:2 and *Yeroushalmi, Shekalim* 6, 1.

9. For example, in *Sukkah* 6b and in *Sanhedrin* 4a.

10. *Midrash Rabbah*, Num. 13:5.

11. *Eruvin*, 13b.

12. It is with the same reservations—relatively speaking—that I undertake this study, which necessarily turns, by its very goal, toward an alteration of the original multiplicity.

13. *Baraitha* by Rabbi Yishma'el.

14. *Baraitha* by Rabbi Eliezer b. Yosé the Galilean.

15. Joseph Heineman, *Aggadah and Its Development* (Jerusalem: Keter, 1974), introduction. We should emphasize that this ambivalence poses problems for "positivist" academic criticism.

16. *Pesahim*, 66a. See chap. 2, pp. 55, 57.

17. *Pirket Avoth*, 5, 26. [Exegesis "turns over" the text as one turns over the earth, to reveal something hidden beneath it. —Trans.]

18. I shall try in this way to set aside the difficulty of a strictly linguistic evaluation of the text or of its levels of language, of which, in exegetical principle, there is no objective measure.

19. Redundancy will be understood—here as well as later in this study—in its usual rhetorical sense of a defective superfluity in discourse and not in the linguistic sense of an overdetermination of information.

20. Rabbi Meir Leibush ben Ye'hiel Mikhel (Russo-Polish frontier, 1809–Kiev, 1879).

21. Introduction to his commentary on Leviticus.

22. The *Tanna'im* are the Masters of the Mishnah (approximately second century).

23. *Yerushalmi, Rosh Hashanah,* 1, 1.

24. *Berakhoth* 31b.

25. Gen. 15:13.

26. In the history of exegesis, the school of Rabbi Akiva, by the number of its adherents, remains predominant.

27. Malbim, *Ayeleth Hashahar*, 150.

28. Ibid., 212.

29. See *Midrash Rabbah*, Gen. 1:1.

30. Rabbi Joseph Gikatilla, *Sha'aré Orah*, new edition (Jerusalem, 1960), chap. 1; see chap. 3, n. 24.

31. In the general sense of the term.

32. These four traditional levels of interpretation emerge from familiarity with the texts and cannot be given a univocal definition. A more detailed presentation from the particular point of view of our inquiry will be found in the course of this study.

CHAPTER 1

1. Here we will not go into the academic discussions regarding the notion of reference, in particular in the case where the object referred

to is an abstract entity. We will limit our discussion to a few simple, operational definitions, whose theoretical and terminological foundations will not be questioned.

2. Leonard Linsky, *Referring* (London: Routledge and Kegan Paul, 1967), 23. See also P. F. Strawson, "On Referring," *Mind* 59 (1950): 320–344. [Translator's note: to preserve this distinction, which is crucial to Rojtman's argument, the word *sens* will be translated throughout as "sense."]

3. For a more detailed discussion, see the article "deictics" in Oswald Ducrot and T. Todorov, *Encyclopedic Dictionary of the Sciences of Language* (Baltimore: Johns Hopkins University Press, 1979), 252. The vocabulary of *deixis* changes according to the discipline (logical or philosophical) and the scholar who is discussing it. Thus one finds the terms "shifters" (Jakobson), "deictics" (Fillmore, Ducrot), and "indicators" (Benveniste) as well as "indexicals" (Peirce), "token-reflexive words" (Reichenbach), or "egocentric words" (Russell).

4. Hans Reichenbach, *Elements of Symbolic Logic* (New York: Macmillan, 1947), 284.

5. Emile Benveniste, *Problems in General Linguistics*, trans. M. R. Meeks (Coral Gables: University of Florida Press, 1971), 220.

6. See note 3 above.

7. Bertrand Russell, *An Inquiry into Meaning and Truth* (New York: Norton, 1940), chap. 7, "Egocentric Particulars," 134. Russell continues: "It does not seem equally feasible to take some other egocentric word as fundamental and define 'this' in terms of it. . . . [N]o word of common speech seems capable of replacing it."

8. In linguistics, "anaphoric" designates any term that refers to a reality previously mentioned in the same context. For example, pronouns and demonstrative adjectives can be used as anaphorics. See R. Galissan and D. Coste, *Dictionnaire de didactique des langues* (Paris: Hachette, 1976). Ducrot and Todorov propose a more general definition: "A segment of discourse is termed anaphoric if one must refer to another segment of the same discourse in order to interpret it (even literally)" (*Encyclopedic Dictionary of the Sciences of Language*, 281). The class of anaphorics is thus subdivided into (1) *anaphorics* proper (the segment to which one is referred—the "interpretant"—*precedes* the anaphoric) and (2) *cataphoriques* (the segment to which one is referred *follows*).

9. John Lyons, *Semantics* (Cambridge: Cambridge University Press, 1977), 2:648.

10. The term is proposed by E. Benveniste.

11. Emphasis supplied by Rojtman. Rojtman quotes the Bible mainly in the French rabbinical translation, introducing slight modifications when a more literal translation is required; to preserve the features she is discussing, I have retranslated from the French, while following as closely as possible the English version in *The Torah: The Five*

Books of Moses, 2d ed. (Philadelphia: Jewish Publication Society of America, 1967). —TRANS.

12. This polyvalence explains the various translations of the word *zeh* in a given context. Respecting the diversity of formulations, we will note between parentheses each occurrence of the term in Hebrew.

13. *Hebräische Grammatik* (Halle: Rengersche Buchhandlung, 1813). *Gesenius Hebrew Grammar*, ed. and enlarged by E. Kautzsch and A. E. Cowley, 2d ed. (Oxford: Clarendon Press, 1910).

14. For a detailed analysis, see Gesenius, p. 442, §136a–b; p. 404, §126a–b; p. 109, §34 and p. 442, §136; p. 446, §138g; p. 442, §136c–d.

15. The secondary form *zu* appears only in the poetic style, and usually in place of the relative. See Gesenius, p. 109, §34, rem. 1.

16. For instance, Mireille Hadas-Lebel, *Histoire de la langue hébraïque (des origines à l'époque de la Michna)* (Paris: Publications Orientalistes de France, 1981).

17. For example, see the entry *"zeh"* in Harkavi's *Dictionnaire d'Hébreu et de Chaldéen* (New York, 1913), which itself appeals to the authority of Gesenius and Fuerst and to that of the Russian scholar J. Steinberg's *Dictionnaire étymologique d'Hébreu et de Chaldéen* (Vilna, n.d.). If one consults an earlier Hebrew-French dictionary, that of Sander and Trenel (Paris, 1859), one finds: *"zeh* (feminine *zot*, plural *eleh*): 1. demonstrative pronoun. *This one*, sometimes before a noun and with an interrogative pronoun, for emphasis, etc. 2. relative pronoun, who, which. 3. adverb of place or time."

18. a) *Dictionnaire de Even-Shoshan* (Jerusalem: Hotsaat Kiryath Sepher, 1966; b) *Ozar Halashon Ha'ivrith*, by Ya'akov Cana'ani (Jerusalem: Massada, 1963; c) *Ha'ivrith Hayeshanah Vehahadasha*, by Eliezer Ben-Yehuda (Jerusalem and Berlin, 1908; Tel Aviv, 1959); d) Yehuda Gur (Tel Aviv: Dvir, 1950).

19. We might also mention the special case of the *Ozar Halashon Ha'ivrith*, the only dictionary among those consulted that notes a specific referent of *zeh*: "In poetry, a term that refers to God."

20. See pp. 17–18, above.

21. See Gur and Harkavi.

22. Konrad Ehlich, *Verwendungen der Deixis beim sprachlichen Handeln, linguistischphilosophische Untersuchungen zum Hebräischen deiktischen System* (Frankfurt-am-Main: Peter Lang, 1979).

23. See especially chapters 6 and 7 of Ehlich's monograph.

24. This text is found in a fasciscle of "Abstracts" by Ehlich.

25. This conceptual aspect of the referential object leads us to prefer the more abstract term "reference" to the more classical term "referent," which generally designates the *real* object indicated by the demonstrative. It is also the term adopted by French translators of Frege.

26. See above, Introduction.

27. *Torah Or* [commentary by Malbim] on *Sifra, Zav* 23.

28. The great classic collections of Midrash we shall refer to include *Midrashé Halakhah*, juridical in character (*Mekhilta* on Exodus, *Sifra* on Leviticus, *Sifré* on Numbers and Deuteronomy) and *Midraché Aggadah*, primarily moralizing (chiefly, *Midrash Rabbah, Midrash Tanhuma*, and the *Yelkutim*). These texts are generally difficult to date, and the most ancient of them go back to the tannaitic period (c. 2d century C.E.).

29. See *Avoth* 5, 26.

30. In the example cited, Midrash sees in the word *zeh* uttered by Esau an allusion to his revolt against God. See chap. 2.

31. *Sifré*, Num. 41 L 8 and 24 L 4, on Num. 5:29 and 6:21. The division of the *Sifré* into pages and lines follows Horovitz's critical edition: *Siphre D'be Rav Fasciculus primus: Siphre ad nomeros adjecto Siphre zutta* (Leipzig, 1917).

32. *Yoma* 4a. In this precise case, the feminine pronoun *zot* refers by allusion to other arrangements necessary for the High Priest's entry into the sanctuary, and which are based on a feminine symbolics. (See chap. 2.)

33. See particularly the midrashim based on Exodus 32:4: "Eleh Eloheha Israel," Here is your God, Israel. See Zohar, B 236b. The traditional edition of the Zohar (Vilna, 1882) is divided into three parts: A for Genesis, B for Exodus, C for the three books of Leviticus, Numbers, and Deuteronomy. We have also indicated the notation by section (*parasha*), page, and paragraph in the annotated edition of the *Sulam* (Jerusalem, 1945–1960) by Rabbi Yehudah Leib Ashlag (Warsaw, 1886; Tel Aviv, 1955). For example, in the notation of the *Sulam* the passage quoted here is indicated thus: Zohar, *Pekudé*, 100, 308.

34. See n. 27, above.

35. *Torah Or.*

36. Let us nevertheless observe that, since the two formulas "today" and "this day today" exist concurrently, no purely linguistic norm allows us to privilege one usage as "marked" with respect to the other, or to conclude, given the equivalence of the turns of phrase, that they have any sort of semantic specificity: it is the *ideological* principle of the economy of expression, as we have defined it in the introduction, that leads commentary to reject this indifferentiation in the utterance and to invest the most complex formula with a surplus of information in comparison to the simplest formula, morphologically the most *economical*, considered as fundamental and normative.

37. *Torah Or.*

38. *Torah Or.*

39. Rabbi Shelomo ben Yizhak (Troyes, 1040–1105), one of the greatest posttalmudic authorities.

40. It seems that this stage is characteristic of "halakhic" jurispru-

dence, although it also includes numerous *Midrashé Aggadah* that are homiletic or parabolic in nature. (See p. 23, above.)

41. See, for a restrictive reading of the expression, Rashi's commentary (Deut. 31:11), based on the Gemara *Sotah,* 41a. *Midrash Rabbah* develops this same interpretation on the basis of another verse in which *zeh* occurs (designating the "book" of the Torah) with the restrictive sense: "At the moment when the Lord revealed himself to Joshua, he found him reading the *Mishneh Torah* [= Deuteronomy] . . . in application of the verse: 'This book (*hazeh*) of the Torah must not leave your mouth'" (*Midrash Rabbah,* Gen. 6:9).

As for the value of specification, Maimonides indicates, following the Mishnah (*Sotah,* 7, 1), that the public reading of the Torah must be made *in Hebrew,* "according to the text of the verse: 'You shall read this Torah (*hazot*) in its original language'" (Maimonides, *Yad Hazakah, Sefer Korbanoth, Hilkhoth Hagigah,* 3, 5).

42. The Pessah Sheni (literally, Second Passover) represents a new opportunity to bring the paschal sacrifice, *with a month's delay,* to anyone who might find himself in a state of impurity *on that very day.* The prescription formulated in the verse ("And you will hold it [the paschal lamb] in reserve until the fourteenth day of this month") is thus applicable—strictly speaking—only to *the month of Nisan proper,* the month of the exodus out of Egypt according to the Jewish calendar, and cannot be extended to the *deferred* celebration represented by the Pessah Sheni.

43. The division of the *Sifra* into pages follows I. H. Weiss's edition (Vienna, 1862).

44. These cases illustrate rather well the notion of "textual *deixis*" set forth above.

45. Rashi explains: "Although she was legally united with him, she has had intercourse with another man."

46. Pages and lines in *Sifré* Deuteronomy according to Finkelstein, *Siphre ad Deuteronominium H. S. Horovitzii & schedis usis cum variis lectionibus et adnotationibus* (New York, 1969).

47. Barukh Halevi Epstein (Pinsk, 1860), *Torah Temimah,* a collection of midrashim accompanied by notes on the Torah. Rabbinical Hebrew customarily designates exegetes by the title of their work. The author of the commentary *Torah Temimah* is thus referred to elliptically as *"Torah Temimah."*

48. The commentary goes further, arguing from this use of *zeh* to demand that witnesses *recognize* the accused, in a process of pedagogical intimidation that is supposed to be carried out in several stages. See below, "Recognition."

49. I owe the elucidation of these complex phenomena to the kindly sagacity of Oswald Ducrot.

50. See note 8, above.

51. Certain coincidences between the syntactical and semantic forms of autonomization must be acknowledged. Beyond a methodological division, both forms simultaneously provide, to different degrees, both types of information (signalizing and thematic).

52. Used most often in such turns of phrase, *zeh* informs us concerning a particular procedure of the ritual. In a general manner, most of the examples of "signalization" are found in the *Midrash Halakhah* (see n. 28, above), which is perhaps more focused on the specific functioning of the sense.

53. One might nevertheless say that it is indeed the ritual as such or the commandment as such that is the subject of the restriction. There would then be a "deixization" (actualization) of these concepts, which are detached from the context of the immediate utterance and considered as existential experience.

54. If this vow concerns him directly, and if he is present at the moment when the commitment is made.

55. Following Austin, one can say that the illocutionary act of freeing someone from a vow must be "felicitous," i.e., carried out exactly and solely by the person qualified to perform it.

56. The division of the *Mekhilta* into pages and lines follows Horovitz and Rabin, *Mechilta d'Rabbi Ismael cum variationibus et notationibus* (Frankfurt, 1931).

57. In this example, the commentary plays on a lexical ambivalence, the root of the word *mass* (*miKShaH*, all one piece) coinciding with that of *difficulty* (*KaSHeH, nitKaSHaH*).

58. See also, on Num. 8:4, *Menahoth* 29b; on Lev. 11:29, *Menahoth* 29a; and on Lev. 11:2, *Hulin* 42a.

59. Here it is the whole of the verse that seems superfluous. This example could also be classified among the cases of "inadequation" (see below).

60. We may acknowledge a parallel reading that makes the word *book* (and the associated thematic sequence) the pivot of the Midrashic interpretation.

61. This reading presents us with a classic effect of "specialization."

62. Halakhah: the jurisprudence of the religious law.

63. Let libertines and rebels not be alarmed: the Talmud itself bears witness to the theoretical character of a case "which has never occurred."

64. Midrash Rabbah, ed. A. M. Mirkin (Tel Aviv: Yavneh, 1968), 143.

65. The latter is founded on the verb *see* in the verse.

66. The literal formulation is more subtle: each one "pointed his finger" (without a complement) in an indirect designation.

67. See Exod. 33:18.

68. Rabbi Hai Gaon, quoted by Tosafoth, on *Gitin* 2a.

CHAPTER 2

1. See Introduction, pp. 11–12, above.

2. Let us recall here, and this remark should be extended to the terminology used in the whole of this chapter as well as in the following ones, that we have not intended to enter into the philosophical consequences of a distinction between "sense" and "reference" in the case of an abstract entity—a discussion (or confusion) that has remained pragmatic for us, and which does not affect our subject, at least before we arrive at our conclusion.

3. See chap. 1, n. 8, above.

4. For the study of the kabbalistic procedure properly so called which can be glimpsed behind these audacities, see chapters 3 and 4.

5. *Naftulé Elokim*, a commentary on the exegetical work of R. Bahyé by R. Naftali ben Eli'ezer Trivesh (Heddernheim, 1546). This gloss is reported by the *Sefer Erké Hakinuyim*, by R. Yehiel ben Shelomo Halperin (Dürrenport, 1806).

6. *Ir Giborim*, a commentary on the Torah (Basel, 1580), by R. Shelomo Ephra'im, Luntschitz (1550–1619). "Ba'al Oleloth Ephra'im." This gloss is reported by the *Sefer Erké Hakinuyim*, by R. Yehiel ben Schelomo Halperin (Dürrenport, 1806).

7. *Zeror Hamor*, an "immediate" reading and the mystical reading of the Torah, by Rav Ephraïm ben Ya'akov Sava Hassefaradi (Spain, d. 1508). Quoted in *Sefer Erké Hakinuyim*.

8. This example is cited *in extenso* and analyzed below.

9. As for the theme of circumcision, its relation to (*zot*) is drawn from a first context. Here is the complete text of the midrash: "Then Moses and the children of Israel shall sing this (*zeh*) hymn to the Lord" (Exod. 15:1). "This hymn: we are made worthy of singing it by purifying ourselves through circumcision. That is why the expression 'this (*zot*) hymn' appears here, where *zot* must be interpreted as designating circumcision, on the basis of the verse: 'Such (*zot*) shall be the covenant which you shall keep: you shall circumcise every male among you (Gen. 17:10)'" (*Midrash Rabbah*, Exod. 23:12).

10. This identification, which is always a bit artificial because of the impossible coincidence of the logical categories of each system, cannot claim exactitude and retains, here as elsewhere, a suggestive character. It nevertheless accounts for a high percentage of the registered phenomena.

11. One might speak of an "anaphorization" of the deictic, to the extent to which the meaning of the passage is to be sought in a preceding occurrence of *Zeh*. The demonstrative would thus operate, in Ehlich's terminology (see chap. 1, pp. 19–20), as a "textual deictic."

12. The textual problems that lead the commentary to explain the particular reference of the demonstrative are of the same order as

those encountered in the preceding chapter, and have no influence on the mode of explication chosen: ambiguity, redundancy, inadequation.

13. In the Warsaw edition, 1876 (vol. 1: Pentateuch; vol. 2: Prophets and Hagiographers).

14. Rabbi Moshe ben Nahman, Nahmanides (Spain, 1194–Palestine, 1270).

15. A division paralleling that established in the first chapter.

16. See Introduction, p. 5.

17. *Gezerah shavah*, a completely original exegetic modality, is generally considered as a subdivision of *Remez*.

18. See chap. 1, "Signalization."

19. The precise determination of the time is itself deduced from a third verse, still located in the same context (Exod. 12:29): "In the middle of the night the Lord struck down all the first-born in the land of Egypt." The plague's cutoff time—midnight—is thus very precisely signified by the expression "that night."

20. Concerning the maintenance of the immediate reading, see T. Todorov, *Symbole et interprétation* (Paris: Seuil, 1978), 120–21.

21. The idea of a hidden motivation of these examples will become more and more pressing as our study progresses. Concerning these precise examples, however, it can provide no more than a general line of reading, without explicit decoding.

22. See chap. 1, "Signalization."

23. Taking into account the restrictions mentioned at the beginning of this chapter regarding the methodological limits of this kind of analysis—which the Kabbalah goes beyond in the direction of a conventional determination.

24. This remark should be connected with what has been said, and what will be said, about the primacy of relation over the content that it conveys. See Conclusion, below.

25. The two stages mentioned here do not correspond to the division chosen for our analysis.

26. But each word of the Torah could serve in its turn as the basis for a new semantic configuration.

27. The technique of contextual memorization thus also leads—and this intuition will be continually confirmed in the following pages—to a concealed systematics. This allows us to better understand its connection with punctual interpretation (which is implicitly conventional), which offers precise referential identifications without passing through the detour of the equivalence of utterances while at the same time arriving at similar results.

28. It seems that in any case the functional *zeh* is usually connected with one of these privileged contexts, paradigm contexts in which the semantic load is the strongest, and which ground the general structuring of the signifieds.

29. Refer to the text cited *in extenso*, p. 55, above.

30. See chap. 1, n. 46, above.

31. Refer, for example, to the logical reduction proposed by *Torah Temimah* concerning another *gezerah shavah* (on the basis of the verse already cited): "And one can account for the fact that the gemara applied the technique of *gezerah shavah* to subjects so distant from one another, through the mere coincidence of terms, by the fact that the expression '*zeh hadavar*' is generally associated only with circumstantial commandments, linked to the particular conditions—the flight from Egypt, etc."

32. One also notes a rather loose semantic contextualization, which argues for the thesis (see below) of an underlying thematic codification.

33. Which would guarantee a transition between the (purely functional) *gezerah shavah* and the punctual determinations recognized by anagogic commentary, of which we have given a few examples at the beginning of this chapter, and which will be more amply elaborated in the following chapter.

34. A kabbalist, the author of a commentary on the Torah; Saragossa, 13th century.

35. See pp. 47–48, above.

36. This verse is generally interpreted by the *Derash* as applying to the Torah (a term that figures explicitly in the Hebraic version), to which man must be prepared to sacrifice his life (whence the metaphorical context of death).

37. It is also interesting to note, before taking up the text itself of the midrash, that the referential determination is produced here in an *indirect* fashion, applying to the most indeterminate case, which is semantically the most undifferentiated.

38. The "merit" connected with Jerusalem is not specified: what counts is the *integration* of the sememe "Jerusalem" into the constellation of the possible "translations" of *zot*.

39. The text itself of the midrash is more concise in its citations, pointing out only the expression in which *zot* occurs and trusting the reader's erudition to decipher the allusions. We have generally cited larger extracts, to facilitate understanding.

40. It can be easily verified that the punctual thematic determinations presented by the Midrash, or suggested by the Kabbalah (see pp. 47–49, above) correspond to a radicalization of the contextual identifications, to a sort of shortcut in reasoning that follows the same semantic lines.

41. This would also explain the certainty manifested in the kabbalistic decoding of meanings, which is explicitly inspired by conventional paradigms. See chap. 3, below.

42. In fact, these two hypotheses (we shall leave their elaboration until later) come together in an essential principle of reading that we

must mention now, and which could be said to found the ideology of Jewish hermeneutics: it acknowledges a relation of superposition (inclusion, intersection, or projection) of the syntagmatic level of the sacred text and the paradigmatic level of the symbolic code connected with it. This principle presupposes a thematic unity *inherent* in the text, which is to be (re)discovered. The postulate of midrashic commentary, tracking down, cutting out, and bringing into intersection with each other referential determinations that are normally arbitrary and contextual, is to recognize in these a coherent internal configuration, by virtue of the particular arrangement of the layers of signification in the text itself. Hence there would be not *triage,* but rather a (pedagogical) exploitation of the contexts. The ambivalence would thus be maintained, since there is both a selection, by the commentary, of privileged contexts that demonstrate a conventional foundation prior to the reading's division of the text (and which guarantees its coherence) and the conviction that there is an *objective* distribution of the contexts in conformity with this division, which Midrash reads and recognizes.

One could also consider in an ambiguous manner—and this ambiguity itself is significant—referentialization by contextual allusion (*Remez*), as determining on the level of the linguistic system a discursive and variable element, which nevertheless reveals *at the same time* an underlying, coded system.

This essential question about whether the text or the system has precedence, which the whole of traditional exegesis leaves unresolved, cannot be truly settled. We shall see later on (chap. 5) that it is resolved by itself. In particular, one might suggest that the holy language, having already produced its entire utterance, tends to merge, asymptotically, system and message.

43. Let us recall that *Peshat* and *Derash* share the first mode, whereas *Remez* covers the second. If exegesis distinguishes these two levels theoretically, many examples, in the traditional coherence itself, remain ambiguous and might be included, according to the angle of hermeneutic perception, into one or another category.

44. See p. 55, above.

45. "One cannot tear a text away from its primary sense" (*Shabbath* 63a).

46. A convergence but not a coincidence: the code itself remains "open" (see chap. 3, below).

CHAPTER 3

1. See chap. 2, p. 48.

2. Value not in the linguistic but rather in the spiritual sense of the term. It represents for the commentator this or that modality of the revelation of the Absolute: hence it is written with a capital letter.

3. If not especially. See the hints throughout this study of a priority of relation over matter.

4. We shall adopt the term "sphere" as a possible translation of *Sephirah*. In spite of its inexactitude, this translation is justified by the phonetic similarity with *Sephirah* and the connotations of "sphere" in English. Beyond its precise sense of "mediation," *Sephirah* presupposes in Hebrew an arithmetical rather than geometrical symbolics (see n. 8, below). For reasons of homography, in this case only we will indicate the phoneme [f] by "ph."

5. Let us recall that *zeh* is already related to a divine principle by the Midrash and the Talmud, on the strength of the expression "this is my God (*zeh Eli*)" (Exod. 15:2).

6. R. Joseph Gikatilla, *Sha'aré Orah*, pp. 27–28. See n. 24, below. In this chapter, the numerous translations of kabbalistic texts generally deviate from their literal sense, retaining only a central theme linked to the perspective of the study. The symbolic of the terms, in their Hebraic formulation, is in fact so precise that any direct transcription, unless it is accompanied by a massive hermeneutic apparatus, necessarily falsifies the spirit.

7. A question that will be left unresolved until the next chapter.

8. The original term *Sephirah*, inexactly translated as "sphere," makes possible an analogous play of meaning, through its connection with the root SPHoR, "to count," and with the idea of number.

9. This structural correspondence with the phenomena of *deixis* is not a matter of indifference, and will be discussed again in the Conclusion.

10. The contents reveal themselves only in the "particular" of each structure, since the Kabbalah as a whole projects onto the world, rather than a definite thematics, geometrical outlines translated from one level to another, and each time named according to the location of their position. The relations between the spheres are only correspondences and homologies that are suddenly *embodied* in such or such a time and in such or such a register.

11. We could see another, no less operational type of structure in this radiating, "star-shaped" arrangement and, acknowledging the reduction of the thematic associations to specific traits of sense, say that they represent a definition "in comprehension" of the sphere and constitute, in spite of the univocal nature of the referentialization, the *sense* of that designation. The conventional and preelaborated character of this structuration (these semantic series are found already constituted in the dictionaries of the Kabbalah) allows us to understand it as a sort of thematic focal point, an overall signified whose common semantic traits, recurring in their diverse crystallizations, lead to an identification of the designated *sphere* as ultimate reference.

12. The Kabbalah acknowledges a semioticization of the created

universe, marking the symbiosis of the real and the sign. See the Conclusion, below.

13. See chap. 5.

14. The *Sephirah* of *Yesod* represents the culmination of the five preceding spheres, of which it is the manifestation. The whole of these six *Sephiroth* receives its name from the most central, *Tifereth*, or splendor.

Zeh, which normally points toward *Yesod*, can thus also refer, by indirect reference, to the first principle of *Yesod*, that is, to *Tifereth*.

15. See R. Joseph Gikatilla, *Sha'aré Orah*, 27–28.

16. R. Moshe Cordovero, *Pardes Rimonim*, Sha'ar 23, "*Sha'ar Erké Hakinuyim*," Perek 7. See n. 24, below.

17. Rabbi Yehiel ben Shelomo Halperin (Russia, 1660–1746), (*Ba'al Seder Hadoroth*), *Sefer Erké Hakinuyim* (Dürrenport, 1806–Roumania 1939).

18. R. Ya'akov-Tzvi Jolles (Galicia, 1778–1825), *Sefer Kehilath Ya'akov* (Otzar Shemoth Pe'alim Vekinuyim Bethorath Rabbi Shimeon Bar Yohai Vekabbalath Ha'ari Hakadosh), Ba'al *Melo Haro'im* (Lemberg, 1870; Jerusalem, 1971).

19. *Kehilath Ya'akov*, entry "*zeh*," p. 18.

20. *Erké Hakinuyim*, "*zot*," p. 263, and "*zeh*," p. 267.

21. Zohar, A 93b (*Lekh Lekha*, 132, 400).

22. As we have hinted, it will turn out that these correspondences, by the structural nature itself of the spheres, are not "closed" but are themselves translated from one register to the other. See pp. 88ff., below.

23. Here the reference, of course, is to the end of History, to the eschatological Salvation.

24. We refer chiefly to the *Sha'aré Orah* (R. Joseph ben Abraham Gikatilla, Spain, beginning of the 14th c.) in the construction of these thematic tableaus, because it offers one of the richest semantic spectrums. The page references are to the Jerusalem edition (1960). To this source we may obviously add the canonical commentary of the Zohar (attributed to Moses of Leon, 13th c.), and also those of R. Bahyé (Saragossa, 12th c.) or Nahmanides (Gera, 1194; Acre, 1270). Various other "lexicons" may also be consulted, such as *Pardes Rimonim* (Rabbi Moshe Cordovero, Spain, 1522; Safed, 1570), or more recently, *Sefer Erké Hakinuyim* (1660–1746, published 1806) and *Kehilath Ya'akov* (1778–1825). These works are true "dictionaries" and offer a nomenclature of key terms with their semantic correspondences in the general system of the kabbalistic "language."

25. Refer to the graph in the preceding section. The kabbalistic tradition moreover recognizes two graphic representations, one linear, the other circular and concentric.

26. Cf. the entries for *zeh* in the *Pardes Rimonim* or the *Kehilath*

Ya'akov. Basing himself on the Zohar (C 160b, or *Shelah Lekha* 25, 72), R. Bahyé also cites concerning the verse "Go that way, toward the hill" (Num. 13:17), the number 12 as one of the secret names of God: "'Go that way (*zeh*)': He tells them the Name corresponding to 12 [represented in the verse by the word]: *zeh,* which has the numerical value of 12."

27. We will have occasion later on to inquire into the nature and functioning of these derivations, which are both logical and conventional. The procedure adopted here is one of thematic coordination within the cultural framework of the Jewish tradition.

28. At least within the perspective adopted.

29. "Israel," the "Written Law," and the "*mitzva*" (commandment) are cited by *Sefer Erké Hakinuyim* as belonging to this same series. *Pardes Rimonim* mentions the same appurtenances (*Tifereth*).

30. Tradition also connects the experience of the sign and the manifestation of God in the universe with the eye as an organ (itself a figure of centrality) and with the sense of sight, as well as the commandments that are linked with them, for example, the threefold annual pilgrimage to the Temple in Jerusalem: "Three times a year, each of your men shall appear in the presence [lit., shall see the face] of the Lord your God" (Deut. 16:16). "And our Sages added: just as he comes to see, he comes to be seen" (*Sha'aré Orah,* 97).

31. [Concerning the *Sephirah* of *Tifereth*]: "Moses alone approached the great Name called the Lord . . . that is why it is written: 'Never again did there arise in Israel a prophet like Moses—whom the Lord singled out, face to face' (Deut. 34:10)" (*Sha'aré Orah,* 121).

32. *Sha'aré Orah,* 58. Its identity is realized in Joseph, the favorite son, the awaited son, the symbolic son (*Sefer Erké Hakinuyim,* entry *zeh,* according to a commentary of *Tsror Hamor,* par. *Vayehi*). *Kehilath Ya'akov* adds to this list the figure of David, and the *Sefer Erké Hakinuyim* adds that of the king-Messiah (based on a commentary of *Ir Giborim, Bo*).

33. It is not surprising to find Moses' rod placed in the grid of derivations evoked by this line (*Sefer Erké Hakinuyim*).

34. Which should be connected with the symbolic number 12 mentioned earlier.

35. Which is limited to the elements mentioned in this study and does not exhaust the other organized "names" of the sphere.

36. See pp. 88ff., below, concerning the possible "displacements" in the referentialization.

37. And, as for *zeh,* their status is ambivalent: they are not experienced by Jewish tradition as merely metaphorical, but also *directly* experienced, actualized, and authenticated in the concrete. See the Conclusion, below.

38. Which motivates in turn new semantic derivations: the seven

levels of holiness, the seven books of the Torah, the seven voices by which it was delivered (*Kehilath Ya'akov*, "*zot*"). The number 7 is found again in the letter Z (*zayin*), the first letter of the word *zot*.

39. One of the Names of God, signifying literally "My Lord," but whose meaning is coded. See n. 46, below.

40. See also *Sha'aré Orah*, 11.

41. In this Law, whose respect is testimony, two particular commandments will be privileged: the one of *circumcision* (Zohar, *Lekh Lekha, Miketz*, and *Vayehi* [A 228a or *Vayehi* 118, 379], *Kehilath Ya'akov*, "*zot*"), which is fundamental in any semantics of the sign (see below), and that of *tefillin*, or phylacteries (*Kehilath Ya'akov*, "*zot*"), which the religious man will "attach to his arm as a symbol and wear on his forehead" (Deut. 6:8).

42. The *Sha'aré Orah* continues: "And this is what Jacob and Esau quarreled about: it is a matter of the right of the first-born [*bekhora*, a permutation of *berakha*, 'blessing'] given by Esau to Jacob. This blessing was then particularized and became the specific heritage of Jacob and his line" (p. 10).

43. The associated thematic *termini*, as they are noted in Halperin's lexicon, include sacrifices, tributes (*terumah*), and tithes.

44. Or by the "mother-cell" of the 12 tribes (*Sefer Erké Hakinuyim*).

45. Whence the Name of *Adonai*, "Lord," to be interpreted in its strict sense as Master-Sovereign.

46. In the kabbalists' vocabulary, this fusion is sometimes rendered by a specific term, the demonstrative pronoun *zu* (neuter in gender and usually employed with the meaning of a relative pronoun): "*zu* represents the union of the two *Sephiroth Yesod* and *Malkhuth.* . . . It is formed by the first letters of the expression: masculine *and* feminine" (*Kehilath Ya'akov*, entry *zu*).

47. "Thus, for example, the prohibition on the mixture of wool and linen is resolved and inverted at the level of the priestly vestments, in which the two materials are mixed" (according to *Yevamoth* 4b, quoted by Elie Munk, *La Voix de la Tora*) (Paris: Fondation Odette Lévy, 1969), 194.

48. Munk, *La Voix de la Tora*, Leviticus, p. 194. Inversely, if the spheres are divided, the forces of evil triumph. The "negative" correspondences that link, for example, *zot* with death or malediction (*Sefer Erké Hakinuyim*) and *zeh* with Satan (*Kehilath Ya'akov*) can be explained in this way.

49. See notes 1 and 46, above.

50. More precisely, it is the infinity of the divine brilliance that marks out on the material of the world the specific limits of each creature; the creature defining his being by the scope of his receptivity itself, as if the living world differentiated itself in accord with the criterion of a spiritual coefficient: "The object that receives the light is

delimited by the light that it receives, and it thereby acquires its norm and its measure" (*Sha'aré Orah*, 52, commentary by R. Matityau Delacrut, a kabbalist and astronomer of the 16th century). The notion of "limit" is here integrated into the very nature of the creature, in its paradoxical reversal: if creation is defined by its inability to cross that limit, it is also in its particular relation to the infinite, and in this relation alone, that each creature affirms its existence. Access to being is realized in the investment of a form by a light—but inversely, the form is itself produced and revealed in the movement of the light that traverses it. See the Conclusion, below.

51. The collection of the *Introductions to the Kabbalah* by Rabbi Yehudah Leib Ashlag is very informative on this subject (*Sefer Hahakdamoth*; see Conclusion, n. 45).

52. On this "deictic" structuration of the system of the spheres, see the Conclusion.

53. An association already inscribed just beneath the surface in the Gemara (*Bava Bathra*, 75b).

54. On the use of the article, see chap. 1, n. 46.

55. However, this does not allow us to disqualify any given author. It is on the contrary the coherence of the reading based on these partial results that must be considered.

Moreover, in this study the dictionaries cited and the precise examples of divergence noted have only a symptomatic value. The semantic schemas established, while founded on "truth," do not claim to be either exhaustive or absolute in locating their units. They only indicate certain lines, the very possibility of identifying them, and the corollary necessity of internal variations.

56. In its turn, this thematics can be transcended and extended in more comprehensive perspectives: the *Kehilath Ya'akov* thus proposes a decomposition of *zot* into three disparate levels: "The word *zot* is formed with the first letters of the three colors: *Zahav* (gold), *Argaman* (scarlet), and *Tekheleth* (azure), which represent respectively the *Sephiroth* of *Binah* [third sphere, feminine, left axis], *Tifereth* [sixth sphere, median axis], and *Malkhuth* [tenth sphere, feminine, median axis]."

57. We shall see that these correspondences are not rigid and also permit internal movement.

58. See n. 24, above.

59. Certain criteria are less clear but are manifested indirectly through the associative operations they make it possible to establish.

60. See notes 40 and 46, above.

61. And generating a coded series based on 6 (or 12) that corresponds to its numerical value in the alphabet.

62. This detour through the letter establishes an ideographic reconstruction of the sense, which will be analyzed in chapter 5, below.

63. See p. 75, above. The numerical value of *zot* appears to be ex-

ploited only in the division of the word into elements (e.g., Z, the mark of the demonstrative, with a value of 7 + O TH, marking the totality), or in its association with other terms (e.g., the preposition *be*, "in," with a value of 2). The total thus comes to 410, an allusion to the duration of the first Temple. See *Midrash Rabbah*, Lev. 21:9, cited by Rashi on Lev. 16:3 (commented on above, pp. 63–64). This disparity between *zeh* and *zot* in the arithmetical analysis underlines its conventional origins.

64. In fact, the fundamental semantic trait "12" can be read directly on the basis of a general notion of concretization, in which the Kabbalah sees the "twelve dimensions" of the real. It thus finds a more immediate semantic derivation that arrays around this number all the signs of the universe, expressing through their valence "12," a single tangible truth. Another combination is possible, which comes back to the number 12 through the numeric value of the vertical "*vav*." We will examine later the concurrence of these techniques of determination, which arrive at convergent results.

65. It should be noted that the matrix-term is not picked out for its particular morphology, but once again chosen by the criteria of signification, which fold this series back on the preceding ones.

66. This explains a change of category in the classification.

67. The reader is referred, for these untranslatable derivations, to the Hebrew text of the *Kehilath Ya'akov* (erekh *zeh* and *zot*).

68. In particular, see chap. 5, p. 132, for the hypothesis that there is a "subtextual" formation of these grids, through which biblical discourse extends the verbal paradigms of each sphere into syntagms. As in the Jakobsonian theory of the poetic message, we find the paradigm by verticalizing these juxtapositions.

69. "It is concerning this blessing (*berakah*) that Jacob and Esau quarreled. It is a question of the birthright (*bekhora*) given to Esau by Jacob" (*Sha'aré Orah*, 9). In the same work there are numerous examples of this double causality. See, e.g., *Adonai* and *Adnuth* (Lordship), p. 9; or *pinah-ponim-panim* (corner-turnaround-face), p. 14, or again *pashot* and *hithpashet* (disrobe-extend), p. 120. In every case, the lexical derivation is accompanied by a thematic motivation. Let us add that in general a priority of the logical coherence given by convention over etymological elaboration of a linguistic nature is recognized. The second series is often given as a "sign," a transformation of the first series, which grounds it in reason.

CHAPTER 4

1. See chap. 1, p. 46.
2. See chap. 2, p. 66.
3. A relation made homogeneous by the recognition of the first theme embedded within each sphere as fundamental "*sense*." These

methodological precautions, which may seem artificial, only aid the presentation, and will disappear in the last part.

4. They are also terminologically designated as "references" on a metaphorical basis.

5. See chap. 3, pp. 71–72.

6. Here again, an exact distinction between signs, signifieds, and references in the case of abstract entities would lead us into philosophical considerations, and even, in the framework of this religious discourse, to metaphysical positions concerning which we do not want to rule until the Conclusion, where some of these uncertainties— within the specific field of Jewish tradition—will be resolved.

7. See chap. 1, pp. 33, 37ff.

8. Thus *Malkhuth* allows, for example, a semanticization as *dor*, "the (present) generation," "since it always resides (*dar*) in Israel" (*Sha'aré Orah*, 90). More generally, see the analyses in the preceding chapter.

9. The whole of the deictic function can be subjected to a single thematic transfer. See chap. 5, pp. 126–127, and Conclusion.

10. See the analysis of "categorial transitivity" in the next chapter, where this relation is specified as "connotation" and as "analogy."

11. See chap. 1, pp. 37ff.

12. Class of signs. See chap. 1, p. 22.

13. With the exception of the determinations derived from a literal equation with a functional character, and whose thematic content is not stable. (See chap. 2, n. 17, on *gezerah shavah*.) However, it ought to be asked, in a more detailed manner and perhaps by subtler means of identification than those used here, whether the coherence brought out is not exercised even in these more formal registers.

14. "The vigor of this (midrashic) exegesis resides not in a literal interpretation, but in a *free* application of the content of the Bible *according to the views and needs of its period*" (Zunz, *Gottensdiestliche Vorträge* [Berlin, 1832], 325; quoted in *Regards sur le Midrach*, by the Grand Rabbi Henri Schilli [Paris: Karen Haseler Vehalimud, 1977], 19). On this widely held thesis, one may also refer to most introductions to Midrash. See, for example, A. Z. Melamed, *Morceaux choisis* (Jerusalem: Kiryat Sepher, 1954), Introduction, 11ff.

15. This hypothesis, which is corroborated by rabbinical sensibility (especially that of the kabbalists) as an ideological principle, could be verified here only by illustration, indicating a new direction of study. A computerized analysis would be required to support it in a rigorous fashion.

16. This phenomenon is particularly noticeable at the level of the *Midrash Aggadah*, which is less dominated by the authority of reasoning than is the *Midrash Halakhah*. See chap. 1, n. 28.

17. Let us recall in this connection that the hermeneutic procedure never appears theorized and does not seem to have any confirmation other than traditional and oral.

18. Let us recall that *zeh* belongs to the sphere of *Yesod* or, more

originarily, to the sphere of *Tifereth*, which governs (and contains) the latter.

19. The transfer of one *Sephirah* on another is a frequent practice and must not handicap the demonstration. See chap. 3, pp. 88ff.

20. See the table summarizing the thematic projections of *zeh* in chapter 3 above.

21. And the grammatical relation between the demonstrative and the reference that it determines in the commentary also becomes less obvious. Each example thus becomes an individual case.

22. Or "linguistic equation." See chap. 2, n. 17.

23. Biblical Hebrew brings together under a single expression, *makom*, the designation of "place" and the Universal Presence animating all places.

24. Moshe Arieh Mirkin, critical edition of *Midrash Rabbah* (Tel Aviv: Yavneh, 1968).

25. More precisely, the *Sephirah* of *Yesod* represents the channel through which the Good flowing from *Hesed* (the fourth sphere) issues forth (*Pardes Rimonim*).

26. A connection strengthened by a verse in Psalms: "This (*zeh*) is the gateway of the Lord, the *just men* will cross through it" (Ps. 118:20). On this type of connection, see chapter 5, Functional Transitivity.

27. In a sense, this argument with floating moorings signals all the more clearly the conventional a priori of the semanticization established. See chap. 2, pp. 47ff., on punctual determination.

28. One can see in this example an implicit *gezerah shavah* based on *zakhor*, "remember," or *yom*, "day." These roots are also inscribed in the anagogic paradigm of *Yesod*.

29. The aleatory character of the juxtaposition proceeds from a discrimination in the selection of themes, which picks out "sea" rather than "rebel" or "miracle."

30. See chapter 3: the spheres, we recall, correspond to forms, and allow contents to pass osmotically between them, especially at the junction point between *Yesod* and *Malkhuth*.

31. Pp. 78, 83, 116.

32. The historians of Jewish hermeneutics did not rule on the play of possible influences between these two branches.

33. The recourse to the now classical terminology of generative grammar is here purely metaphorical.

34. The existence of this pyramid, which orients all the resources of exegesis toward the apex of Sod, is never asserted, but it is indirectly confirmed by tradition.

35. The relation of sense to reference is here considered globally, and in a somewhat metaphorical way.

36. See chap. 2, n. 45.

37. The polemic attitude adopted by F. Rosenzweig and his followers (in the contemporary period, Y. H. Yerushalmi) against the

historical positivism of modern Jewish studies is well known. See F. Rosenzweig, "Rouha Uthkufathah shel Hahistoriah Bayahaduth," in *Neharayim* (Mossad Bialik, 1961), and Yosef Hayim Yerushalmi, *Zakhor* (Seattle: University of Washington Press, 1982).

CHAPTER 5

1. Contextual in the broad sense of the term, since it includes an architecture internal to the utterance and the variable situations of the addressee.

2. The latter say nothing about the register of signification involved but rather distinguish themselves by the relation that generates them. They will found, in a second paragraph, the study of a system of combination of units rather than the understanding, as in this first paragraph, of their semiotic nature itself.

3. Unmotivated in the relationship between signifiers and signifieds, or in a relationship between the sign and a referent that would consider the referent itself a new sign. This arbitrariness—which in linguistics founds cohesion in a system of natural languages and allows the play of interferences between significations—does not, however, exclude the working (in some way poetic) of (relative) a posteriori motivation, in the confrontation between terms and texts. See, on these notions, the paragraph on the arbitrariness of the sign in F. de Saussure's *Course on General Linguistics*, trans. M. R. Meeks (Coral Gables: University of Florida Press, 1971), 67, and the article "arbitraire" in O. Ducrot and T. Todorov, *Encyclopedic Dictionary of the Sciences of Language* (Baltimore: Johns Hopkins University Press, 1979), 130. This first point of view will moreover be combined at the level of Sod with the recognition of a *radical* motivation of all the words in the language, in the term-for-term coincidence of appellation and identity. These positions are contradictory, but the first *does not invalidate* the second, and they are integrated into exegesis in a single hermeneutic whole.

4. Whose relation to the text is itself historically and structurally uncertain.

5. The different definitions of the symbol generally stress a function of *representation* founded on an *analogical* relationship (Lalande). According to Saussure, there always remains within the symbol a rudimentary natural link with what it symbolizes (*Course in General Linguistics*, p. 68). *Symbolization* thus appears most often to be partially *motivated*, and in this it is opposed to the *arbitrary semiotic* functioning of signification, which brings the signifier and the signified together in a single sign. For methodological reasons, we have used the criterion for symbolization proposed by T. Todorov: a "more or less stable [analogical] association between two units at the same level (that

is, two signifiers or two signifieds)" (*Encyclopedic Dictionary of the Sciences of Language*, p. 102).

6. The basic linguistic sign can thus engender at least two symbolic series. We shall see later that it is never erased as such and always presents itself as a sign in a natural language.

7. Todorov, *Encyclopedic Dictionary of the Sciences of Language*, p. 195.

8. From a very different point of view, L. Hjemslev also distinguished several aspects of the signifier. In particular, his distinction between "form" and "substance" could serve our purposes if the perspectives were adjusted.

9. In the same way, R. Moshe Cordovero divides *zot* into "Z" (with a value of 7, corresponding to the 7 superior spheres) and "*eth*," linking the *aleph* with the *tav*, which represents *Malkhuth* (*Pardes Rimonim, Sha'aré Erké Hakinuyim*, entries "*Zot*" and "*Eth*").

10. We should note here the "open" character of the progression of this serial construction. See n. 17, below.

11. See Lyons, *Semantics*, 2:656.

12. Charles Bally, *Linguistique générale et linguistique française* (Bern: Francke, 1944), 79.

13. Lyons, *Semantics*, 2:656–657.

14. Bertrand Russell, *Inquiry into Meaning and Truth*, 135.

15. This "substantialization" of grammatical traits can moreover be extended to the definition of the deictic in the linguistic system: its general characteristic (as actualizer) makes possible semantic transpositions of greater scope, turning directly on the very nature of the last two *Sephirot* and the metaphysical system that bears them: that is, in both cases, on their relational value (see the Conclusion):

a) Its actualizing function accounts on the philosophical level for a possible *incarnation* of values. Through the irruption of an outside into the universe of discourse, through the actual intersection of the real and language, it refers to a thematics of limits and revelation. By its empty form, it also points toward the "open" *Sephirah* of *Malkhuth*, the sphere of ontological availability.

b) The parametric system it establishes makes possible an infinite regress of the selected center of reference: "Admittedly, this zero point [the *hic et nunc* of the context of utterance] is egocentric . . . but its egocentricity is not necessarily subjective. . . . [I]t is simply a matter of convenience that speakers should use the place and time of utterance as part of the point of reference: they might, in principle, use the spatio-temporal location of something else, fixed or variable, in the physical environment" (John Lyons, "Deixis and Subjectivity: *Loquor, ergo sum?*" [New York, 1980], 32).

This systematic reference to an "elsewhere" ultimately sets up an infinite structure whose recurrent formation is respected by anagogy, and which defers the determination of meaning until the spheres whose origin cannot be grasped. Ultimately, it is thus also through its *grammaticality* itself that *deixis* enters into the semantic field of hermeneutic discourse.

16. At the same time a sort of transfer of symbolic categories onto semantic strata is produced: the hierarchy of representations runs along a scale that is ideologically founded in the Kabbalah and moves from the most concrete ("below") to the most immaterial ("above"), and imprisons in writing the conceptual light of hidden truths. This economy has repercussions on the series of connotations: arranged in an order of increasing abstraction, they make us pass from precepts of every life to the disembodied Values of spirituality. This organization of the world, which echoes that of meaning, will be discussed again in the Conclusion.

17. However, we should recall that these networks, although structurally defined, are incomplete in the projections they allow. This reductive schematism, which is necessary for the argument, will be transcended in the Conclusion.

18. In the Conclusion this consideration of an extrasemiotic reality, which complicates the play of correspondences, and which is not homogeneous with the initial data of the study, will be included in the recognition of a general semioticization of the living.

19. On the side of the sign "good," the sequence is extended by new contextualizations, for instance: "Say of the 'just man' that he is 'good'" (Isa. 3:10).

20. Let us recall that several centuries after the constitution of the canonical Midrash, the written Kabbalah borrows from the latter its forms of writing and reproduces its models.

21. See chap. 2, p. 48.

22. Generally, the hierarchical relationship between the mystical tradition and the text is ambiguous. Some schools come down in favor of the priority of the oral over the written. This option is corroborated by the testimony of contemporary kabbalists. (Yeshivat *Sha'aré Shamayim,* Jerusalem).

23. A linguistic basis itself founded on a conventional identification, since *Malkhuth,* never appearing *as such* in the text, is always represented in the text, through a coded symbolism, as one or another linguistic term.

24. Numerous examples of the same type, not necessarily bearing on the demonstrative, dot the kabbalistic commentaries. See, among other examples, pp. 13 (on *kol,* "the totality") and 14 (on the Temple) of the *Sha'aré Orah.*

25. The expression is J. L. Austin's (*How to Do Things with Words,* 2d ed. [Cambridge, Mass.: Harvard University Press, 1975], lecture 8), and refers to the production of a linguistic signification by an utterance.

26. The terminology used suggests reference to the Jakobsonian theory of the poetic function.

27. An ambivalence that the positivist critic reduces to circular-

ity, to the extent that the kabbalistic gridding seems to him logically and chronologically posterior to the effects of meaning tracked by the Midrash.

28. *Sha'aré Orah*, Introduction, 3; Zohar C 73, or *Aharé Moth* 103, 296.

29. The loss of the referential mobility characterizing *deixis* appears all the clearer here because Sod challenges the absolute values that normally exclude a punctual relation to the present moment of utterance, to the actuality of existence.

30. We leave at the same time the Jakobsonian perspective that limits itself to the analysis of a mechanical phenomenon ("contiguity") of projecting the paradigm onto the syntagm. The syntagmatic relation between elements of the paradigm *is organized* grammatically here, and articulated in definitions, in contrast with the Jakobsonian projection, which is syntactically inert.

31. See Zohar C 145b, or *Naso* 205, 143.

32. On *Vezoth Haberakhah* (Deut. 33:1). See chap. 3.

33. This confusion of *langue* and *parole*, of a particular utterance and a linguistic system, is also based on the idiolectic character of the Bible, which presents itself as a unique message, the single manifestation of its own code. See the Introduction, above.

34. The first levels of exegesis opt for an inductive approach, starting from an indefinite demonstrative that is determined in context: the word *zeh* represents the unknown, gradually illuminated by the references it determines. But *zeh* can be grasped vertically, and in an inverse movement, as the specific appellation of *Yesod*. This proper reference thus makes possible a distribution of meaning into the utterances in which it appears (inversion of the determination). A priori full of occult signification, it illuminates and conditions its contextual references.

35. Lvov edition (Lemberg), 1865.

36. The sememe "blessing" already appears as a thematic terminus in a literal reading at the first level (*Peshat*), recapitulating the particular contents of the blessing given by Jacob to his children.

37. R. Ya'akov ben Asher, "Ba'al Haturim" (Germany 1270–Toledo 1340).

38. A neighboring midrash, which does not bear directly on *zot*, adopts the same technique: see *Midrash Rabbah*, Deut. 8:2.

39. The choice of this precise context, which is both rich and easily accessible, is obviously didactic. Other inventories would give equivalent results. One could for example refer, for the example of Leviticus (16:3), to the following commentaries: *Midrash Rabbah*, Lev. 21; *Midrash Rabbah*, Exod. 38:8; *Midrash Rabbah*, Num. 18:21; *Tanhuma*, Num. 23; *Sha'aré Orah*, p. 27; Zohar C 8b, 31a, 37b (or *Vayikra* 40, 114, *Tzav* 35, 99, and *Shemini* 12, 37), etc. The following verses can also serve as a basis for a more complex hermeneutic development: Gen. 2:24; Exod. 15:1; Lev. 6:2.

40. The expositions of the Kabbalah in particular have the habit

of developing, in the course of their commentaries, different textual landmarks that all lead, by way of distinct derivations, to the same assertions. See for instance the exegeses on the exile of the *Shekhinah* (Presence): Lev. 26:44; Ezek. 1:1; Ps. 119:50.

CONCLUSION

1. Moreover, only a metaphorical expression could account for these ungraspable truths.

2. See the following note.

3. This is the *Tsimtsum,* or founding withdrawal. See the *Sefer Maftehei Hokhmath Ha'emeth,* by Rabbi Sha'ul Beuman (Warsaw, 1937; Jerusalem, 1977), 22, siman 3 and 4.

4. See *Sefer Mafte'hei Hokhmath Ha' emeth,* siman 10.

5. The *Adam Kadmon,* which proceeds directly from the *En Sof,* represents a sort of generic milieu that permits the emergence of words and recapitulates them in itself (see *Ozeroth Hayim,* ed. Mekor Hayim, Jerusalem: *Sha'ar Ha'igulim,* 1a). Situated at the point of articulation with the primordial Infinite, it is generally excluded from the calculus of the derivations.

6. This traditional division returns, with variants and shifts of level, from the Zohar to the Lurianic classification, in all introductions to the Kabbalah. See, for example, the collection of Rabbi Yehuda. Leib Ashlag (see chap. 1, n. 33), *Sefer Hahakdamoth* (Jerusalem: Kabbalah Research Center, 1974), Preface to the Zohar, 95, pars. 4 and 6; or *Sefer Mafte'hei Hokhmath Ha'emeth,* 36, siman 12.

7. Preface to the Zohar, p. 95, par. 7.

8. See chap. 3, p. 73.

9. See n. 6, above.

10. The details of these correspondences will be found on p. 99 of the Preface to the Zohar, par. 23.

11. See, for example, the *Kuntres Kelalé Hathalath Hahohkmah,* based on the commentaries of the Gaon of Vilna and R. Moshe Haïm Luzatto (Warsaw: Schuldberg, 1893; Jerusalem, 1969).

12. A metaphor that will prove to be not fortuitous.

13. If one admits a philosophical definition of *deixis* whose primordial function would be to "change the virtual into the actual," there looms here a functional correspondence that motivates the metaphor used, and lays the foundation of an identification of the structures of the real with those of sense.

14. We recall in this regard the structural doubling of the deictic, which is simultaneously oriented, by the very definition of its sense, toward the code (symbolic function) and toward *praxis* (indexical function). This ambivalence thus places it at the center of a study on the double location of signification and gives it an emblematic value in the broadening of these data to a metaphysical iconicity.

15. The thesis of an original Text (the Torah), which is the first principle of Creation, is developed by certain post-Lurianic kabbalists. See Israël Saroug (born in Egypt at the end of the 16th c.), *Limoudei Aziluth* (Lvov, 1850). The Midrashic version of this reversal is well known: God, ready to create the world, consults the Torah to find the ineffable, infallible law of its structure (*Midrash Rabbah*, Gen. 1:1).

16. The initials of *Aziluth, Beriyah, Yezirah, Asiyah*. The acronym is proposed by the kabbalists themselves.

17. See, e.g., infra, n. 21.

18. *Ba'al Hatanya* insists on this distinction: see *"Sha'ar Hayihud Veha'emunah,"* chap. 7, "Vehineh Mikan," and chap. 46.

19. Thus Moses, hidden in the crevice of the rock, spelling out in his cry the *attributes* of God: "Then I shall withdraw my hand and you shall see me *from behind*; but my Face cannot be seen" (Exod. 33:23).

20. See Rabbi Ashlag, Preface to the Zohar, p. 97, par. 12.

21. The borrowing is metaphorical here, to the extent that Saussure situates his analysis in a purely linguistic field. It is, however, Saussure to whom we owe the recognition of the principle, developed by the structuralist tradition, of a *differential* and *negative* apprehension of the elements of a system.

22. This is the double structuration presented above.

23. *Talmud Eser Sephiroth*, p. 46, par. 2.

24. The maxim is cited by Rabbi Shelomo Alkabez, in his liturgical poem "Lekha Dodi." (For the metaphysical application, see Preface to the Zohar, p. 99, par. 23.)

25. This paradox is conveyed by the *Sephirah* of *Malkhuth*, the lowest, the most distant from the primitive illumination, but *at the same time* the most complete, the closest to the initial Will. Thus it is no accident that its generic theme is that of the receptacle, that is, the mark of an availability for fulfillment. The more the consciousness of absence is acute, the more the capacity of presence. The more sensible the lack, the more profuse the light that fills it. Nor is it an accident that this *Sephirah* is represented in language by an *empty* term, the demonstrative.

Our study has in fact brought out the selective semantic fixation of the fundamental biblical symbols on the variable that is *least* full of sense, on the chameleon-category of *deixis*. In this centrality of the shifters—and grammatical words in general—there is a deliberate ideological choice: at the opposite pole from a substantialist theory of description in Russell's manner ("Egocentric Particulars"), which for example makes of the demonstrative a sort of superfluous determinant, the Hebraic understanding concentrates the most intense weight of signification on the "openness" of deictics.

More generally, anagogical commentary sees in the Torah a statement of the *Shemoth* or divine attributes, that is, the revelation of the Infinite in some particular *modality* (see chap. 5, n. 28).

26. This convergence of signs is thus applicable to consciousness in action. This is a correlation that Hebrew calls Halakhah, the progress of the Law "on the move," or jurisprudence. By adjusting the code to the real, the Halakhah in turn builds a bridge between incompatible functions whose ambivalence it maintains. In the mystical (Hasidic) understanding, the homology is reversed: each act accomplished in the overflowing of the concrete goes back to the source of its necessity and modifies the structural equilibrium of the superior worlds.

27. This is the mystical, simultaneously metaphysical and moral thesis of the *Teshuva* (Return) defended by Rabbi Kook in his *Oroth Hateshuvah* (Jerusalem, 1925).

28. "Rabbi Akiva teaches: All is foreseen *and* freedom is given" (*Avoth*, 3, 19).

Index

Page numbers in italics refer to tables.

Printed in the United Kingdom
by Lightning Source UK Ltd.
124062UK00002B/1-3/A